"You Can Use Yellow for Leaves"

Odyssey of an African-American Professor

by

Charles V. Hamilton

path press
ORIGINAL & REPRINT PUBLISHERS

Library of Congress Cataloging-in-Publication Data

Names: Hamilton, Charles V., author.
Title: "You Can Use Yellow for Leaves" : Odyssey of an African-American Professor / by Charles V. Hamilton.

Description: First edition. | Evanston, Illinois : Path Press, Inc., 2017. Identifiers: LCCN 2017040947 | ISBN 9780910671163

Subjects: LCSH: Hamilton, Charles V. | Hamilton, Charles V.--Childhood and youth. | African American college teachers--Biography. | African American civil rights workers--Biography. | African Americans--Illinois--Chicago--Biography. | African Americans--Social conditions--20th century. | African Americans--Illinois--Chicago--Social conditions--20th century.

Classification: LCC LA2317.H385 A3 2017 | DDC 378.1/982996073--dc23
LC record available at https://lccn.loc.gov/2017040947

Printed and bound in USA
First Printing November 2017

Path Press, Inc.
Bennett Jones Johnson
pathpressinc@aol.com
(847) 492-0177
P.O. Box 5683
Evanston, IL 60204 United States

DEDICATION

I dedicate this book to the memory of my wife Dr. Dona C. Hamilton, my wife of 60 years and my daughter, Carol L. Hamilton, who died at age 37 in an airplane crash in South Africa.

In their own personal ways they taught me how to be a spouse and father. Since each role involved many twists and turns, ups and downs, each of them showed me how to adapt, to persist, to consent (seemingly more than I thought necessary), but above all—as a family. When times were a bit rough, we could always use yellow for leaves.
I miss them so.

Contents

ACKNOWLEDGMENTS

A book such as this obviously owes an acknowledgment to all those I write about in the text. If they were around to read it now I can imagine how each would react—a raised eyebrow, a smirk, a frown, a tilted head of disagreement, a tear, a smile. I owe them all my deepest gratitude.

Each in her and his own way taught me how to grow, learn, cope, and above all to care about others. Therefore, in a real sense, they are all the co-authors of this book.

I am also pleased to acknowledge the DuSable Museum of African American History in Chicago. this historical institution has graciously established the Charles V. and Dona C. Hamilton Research and Study Institute and will provide facilities for archival, study, and forums for research for scholars and others interested in the subject of African American history.

In the final stage, I must acknowledgment the contribution of Lila Goldston. A friend, she read and typed my handwritten pages. (Full disclosure) I have never learned to compose on anything but pencil and paper. And my penmanship was not one of my few skills. Therefore, she was invaluable—and patient. I am fortunate and grateful.

You Can Use Yellow for Leaves
Introduction

I always wanted to "write down" what I heard and saw – growing up in Muskogee, Oklahoma and Southside Chicago during the "great depression." My mother moved with her 3 children to Chicago in 1935. Our father had, I thought and was then told "deserted" the family. (Not true.) I found out 50 plus years later, when government records showed that he had been "arrested" several times for "bootlegging!" (Not deserted.) I only found out when President Jimmy Carter appointed me to the National Council of Humanities.

On my application I responded "no" to the question whether any parent had been arrested or a member of the Communist party. A Government search revealed that I had lied: my father had been arrested several times in Oklahoma for "bootlegging." He was in and out of jail – not deserting! How was I to know that.

I think later I was more concerned about why my family kept this information from me than I was about the fact of his jailing. I came to assume there was an intent to conceal from embarrassment or to protect from "bad" behavior. It was never discussed in family gatherings or among my many cousins. All my mother's five brothers were full-time workers with steady jobs. They became the "male models" (a term we certainly did not use then) in my life.

They were <u>always</u> ready to help their sister –my mother. My mother's sisters were letter writers. They constantly kept in touch by mail – from Los Angeles, Detroit – wherever. (Penmanship was prized and some probably never finished high school.)

My early years in Chicago were a mixture of pleasure, poverty, listening, learning, and above all "writing" down things. Little jokes we youngsters told each other, big discussions on "What do you want to be when you grow up." Things like that, famous black people who were "fighting for the race." Or, of course, popular athletes and entertainers. "Our" heroes.

In my case, I also always heard one major piece of advice: "First, get your education." Frequently followed by something like: "They can never take that away from you."

My buddies and I clearly knew who "they" were. All this was part of my every-day life.

These vignettes start there.

Sound advice, but I did not understand it as such. I thought it was like, "eat all your food so you can grow up healthy."

I grew up listening, writing poems, stories, and hoping to be a writer "when I grow up" for the Chicago Defender or Pittsburgh Courier. As things developed, I wound up becoming a university Professor, getting involved in the burgeoning "civil rights movement" in the South and North, and naively taking risk to career, family, safety and FBI suspicion.

Along the way, some would say I overdid the "get your education" advice, receiving a B.A., J.D. law degree, M.A., and Ph.D. in that order from 1951-1964. Fired from one teaching job (Tuskegee University) and 20 years later being given an honorary degree by that school, I was becoming a "controversial" academic activist. The vignettes in this book tell part of that journey. (At least seven books, one co-authored with Stokely Carmichael (Kwame Toure), another with my wife of sixty years, Dr. Dona C. Hamilton.) I easily assumed that combining academic research and political participation was a natural thing for me to do. I could never have been satisfied with just learning and teaching. I had to also be doing....

For this reason, I soon became a "controversial" person. I certainly did not see the title (it was once referred to as "infamous"), but it became clear that if one strayed too far from the accepted scrip of protest and struggle, there would be trouble ahead. Namely, being labeled a "communist," or of "hating whites," or heaven forbid, accused of "advocating violence." All these appellatives were there for the taking. And, to many of my friends (and some family), they were sufficient to warn me constantly to "play it safe."

I appreciated the concern and understood it came from those who honestly cared. There was no mistaking that. And this is, I hope, one of the most important features of this series of vignettes.

They represent my early years of a caring family, keeping in touch, constantly writing letters, checking on each other. They also reflect the personal attention of a teacher who took time on her own – outside the classroom – to tutor me. (No grant money caused her to do that. No special rules from a far distant school board.) These are vignettes of a "community," steeped in poverty, racial bigotry, many on "relief" as was my family for a time, able to develop a communal spirit and common joy in moments of shared "victory" and casual talk. When "Joe won," <u>we</u> won. There was protection and comfort in such an otherwise <u>Northern</u> environment. One learned to respect and enjoy one's own kin, kitch, and kind. Later, when I and other Black Power advocates were labeled "Black Separatists" with implications of being against "integration," I simply concluded (privately but comfortably) "before we can enter the (so-called) open society, <u>we</u> must first close ranks."

I reflect now how important such an early environment was even though the "outside" world was telling us we were "inferior," "not ready," "not good enough to compete."

In an interesting way, growing up in South Side depression era–Chicago gave me a strength I did not then recognize or understand. My family, my minister, my teachers were telling me I could not only be "as good as" anybody else, but I could be "better."

They never put it quite that way, because, quite frankly, that would have been considered "boastful" and arrogant.

In those times, we used the term "equal." We wanted to be "treated equally." Fair enough. And still a laudable goal. But these vignettes have challenged me to think beyond that laudable goal. If I only seek to be "equal" to "them," I might settle for being "like" them. And quite frankly, that is not enough.

Growing up in that environment, there were family, neighbors, friends who served as some of my best "professors" who never went to college. They were character-builders with credentials of caring, ambition for us children, honesty. I soon really wanted quite early to make them proud of what they had done.

This was the reason I am convinced in my own case, I never had a feeling of inferiority. I did not need a "black power" movement to tell me I was "black and proud." I grew up in a segregated neighborhood knowing full well that an evil and unjust political system was not what my people caused and maintained.

At the same time I understood that my response should not/need not be one of hatred. I would be like that barber in chair #3 – cool and decisive.

I concluded that Professor John Hope Franklin was right: stop counting. I chose to never start counting to prove what is clearly the laudable goals to achieve.

My interest in the struggle against apartheid in South Africa grew rapidly from my first visit in 1979. I have returned to that country many times since for different reasons. My daughter was killed in an airplane crash with a delegation headed by Secretary Ronald Brown in 1996. She never got her wish. I plan to keep my promise to her.

This was not a casual promise. And it explains why in my retirement years I choose to spend considerable time with an important organization with which she was familiar: Shared Interest, Inc., based in New York, with programs in South Africa and other parts of southern Africa. It supports economic efforts of locals starting their own businesses. Carol would want me to do that. In fact – she would insist.

To be sure, there will be many challenges with which to cope.

Thus, I am constantly mindful of my older brother's calm counsel: "You can use yellow for leaves."

"You Can Use Yellow For Leaves"

It was the thickest coloring book I ever had—before or since—and I had just about finished it all in that one day. That wasn't too hard to do if you spent practically all the time on it, as I did. The pages were not the big size. They were the size of a normal school note book. I think I liked that kind better, but I'm not sure why.

I had gotten up early before it was really light outside; it was Christmas morning in 1936. There was no snow and it was raining a little and not too cold. I knew it would be a dreary, dark day. But it was Christmas. So, it couldn't be that bad.

I had gone with my Mother to Toyland at the South Center Department Store about two weeks before and told Santa Claus what I wanted—a coloring book and a box of sixteen crayons. Of course, I wanted other things, a red wagon, a toy car (one you could wind and would run on its own), and a baseball glove. My Mother had told us that Santa Claus only was sure to bring one gift. Therefore, we should make certain that we asked for the one we really wanted.

Well, I really wanted the baseball glove, but I sort of knew I wouldn't get that. The wagon was second, but somehow I figured that wouldn't happen either because my Mother would sort of look away slightly whenever I mentioned it. Even then, I figured it cost too much and somehow or other (in a confusing but strangely certain way) I came to realize that there was a connection between Santa, surprises and money. To be sure, you wouldn't get anything if you were "bad," but you also knew not to ask for anything that cost too much money. Although I don't recall money being a subject around our house, when it came to making up Christmas lists. At any rate, I had not sorted out all these things as yet. So I played it safe and told Santa about the coloring book and the box of sixteen crayons.

I was seven and my brother was twelve. Santa Claus was still real enough for me to want to believe in him. Even if there were a few moments doing the year and a few discussions in the backyard with the other kids in the neighborhood to plant a few seeds of doubt. Anyway, there was no need to take unnecessary risks. If you didn't go to see Santa Claus, who knows what might not happen!

Things had been pretty quiet and unbusy-like around our house the several days before this particular Christmas. My Mother was sick and in bed a lot of the time. There were not the normal season's decorations, a tree, trinkets on the door and the window, dotting our two room kitchenette. My Mother did not bake any pies that Christmas (I always looked forward to the mince-meat pie). There was no big, special dinner that year. I always remember my Mother cooking us a turkey with all the stuffing. The odors of those preparations just consumed our small place and seeped over the transom into the hall and mixed with similar odors coming from the other seven or eight kitchenette apartments on that floor in that four story tenement at 4940 Indiana Avenue.

We usually had a small, but more than adequate Christmas tree that we decorated at least a week before Christmas. I liked it when it snowed because that's the way the picture books portrayed Christmas. Sometimes we would place the Christmas cards we had received from our aunts and uncles and cousins from around the country on the dresser. My Mother would clear a space for this special season. I remember trying to arrange them, so that you could see all the pictures and none would be hidden from view.

But the Christmas of '36 was different. We didn't seem to be going scurrying around, hanging up things, rearranging things and, well, just sort of getting ready and all. On the day itself my Mother spent most of the day in bed, getting up only a couple of times, once to fry the hamburgers for dinner. My two year old sister got a red ribbon and I remember her in bed most of that day next to my Mother.

But when I rolled out of bed, I was as excited as if there was snow and a tree and the odors and the decorations and the mince-meat pie and all. After all, it was Christmas. My brother got up with me; we did our normal Christmas morning ritual of rushing into the other room which served as a combination living room and our Mother's bedroom. I smiled and grinned as I spied the one thing Santa had left. The neatly wrapped two packages were on the chair by the window. The tag said, "To C.V. from Santa." A third package was for my brother Owen. I quickly noticed that there was no extra surprise gift this time. We always got something that we didn't ask for, but not this time, and I promptly forgot about it.

I tore off the wrappings. One was the coloring book. The other was the box of crayons. But I noticed that it was only an eight crayon box. At first I thought Santa made a mistake, leaving the eight crayon box instead of the sixteen crayon box which I had told him I wanted. But it didn't matter. I smiled broadly and held it up for my Mother to see. She was slightly sitting up in bed and weakly raised her eyebrows as if to join in my surprise. I immediately plopped down on the floor by the chair and started in on page one.

My brother, Owen, had opened his package. He had gotten a dark blue sweater and was pulling it on over his head. I remember thinking how sorry I felt that when you got older you only got things to wear. No toys. Anyway, I would get that sweater in a few years, patched and as a hand-me-down. My brother went back into the combination kitchen and our bedroom and started putting away the roll-a-way bed we shared. Then he fixed oatmeal for the two of us. I stopped long enough to eat the oatmeal and to change out of my pajamas. Then I diligently went back to the

coloring book. A little later the dishes were washed and put away.
Then, my brother came and stretched out on the floor nearby and
watched me in my work of art.

I remember asking him if he wanted to color one part of one
picture. I really didn't like that he didn't have anything new to
play with. He just shrugged off the offer with a shake of the head.
It seemed he was almost like a grown-up, so I guess he didn't
mind not having something to play with on Christmas morning.
He just sat there, wearing his sweater, and watched me color
picture after picture.

The sun never came out that day, and we had to keep on one
table lamp. For a while, my brother turned the radio on softly.
Then he just came back and watched me at work. Later, my
Mother got up and cooked the hamburgers and string beans, and
we ate quickly. And I went back to my coloring book.

I could hear some of the other kids in our building, playing with
their new toys out in the long hallway, but I didn't want to join
them. Anyway, the coloring book wouldn't go well with racing
cars and marble shooters. So I just busied myself with page after
page. My Mother asked if I really liked my Christmas present, and
I said something that made her smile as she lay there in bed. I
would study what crayon to use and sometimes my brother would
hand it to me. Then the evening came. I never enjoyed Christmas
evenings. It meant the end of a big, happy day and you had to
wait another whole year.

Occasionally, I would thumb through the remaining pages to
see what sort of pictures were coming up. I had used a lot of
red and blue and brown and green. I was running out of green.
Eight crayons didn't go very far with such a thick book. I began
to wonder again if Santa really misunderstood me. I was sure I
had asked for a sixteen box of crayons. I wondered if he'd taken it
back to the North Pole with him, or if he dropped it off someplace
else by mistake. But at any rate, that eight crayon box wouldn't
last long with only one color per box. I could see that I had a lot of

outdoor pictures left with trees and grass and things like that. And I knew that I was going to run out of green crayon.

I remember mentioning that to my brother. My Mother heard me asking if he thought Santa might just have made a mistake or something. I remember Mother softly asking if something was the matter and I told her I was running out of green crayon.

My brother glanced quickly toward Mother and gave a little nod like he was saying to Mother everything was alright. Then he whispered to me that Santa probably just ran out of the sixteen crayon boxes before he got to our place.

The street car on Indiana Avenue went by every now and then, which was the only movement outside. Our Uncle Zeke, Aunt Lula and our two cousins dropped by for a few minutes. I proudly showed them my coloring book. Nothing else, other than eating, interrupted the day and my coloring. But I just couldn't figure out how Santa made such a mistake.

I can't say it bothered me too much, but I sure wanted to know why. I mentioned it once again to my brother. He had his sweater on and his knees were pulled up to his chest; he just sat there and sort of watched quietly. Again, I thought, I hoped he would get a toy to play with on his birthday in March. A person really should have a toy to play with, and not just something to wear on a special day like Christmas—even an almost teenager like my big brother.

But then I had this more serious problem facing me. I had a big forest picture coming up which would take a lot of brown and green. And I was running out of green!

It was nighttime. My Mother and sister had dozed off. My brother was still sitting on the floor near me. Sort of making sure, it seemed like, that I was okay and didn't need anything. I remember that frequently he did things like that. Like helping me when I had to lift something extra heavy or watching as I walked past a bunch of tough guys in the neighborhood who were always taking money from us smaller ones. Or, like now, making sure I didn't take unnecessary things to my Mother for her to deal with. He could fix things, or at least patch them up a little. And it seems he could always make something out of something else. Like with using a stick pin on a model plane wing or improvising a way to fix a broken skate. I remember he also carefully taught me how to grow and groom "bangs". He knew just how long to let your hair grow and how to get it cut to get good "bangs". He knew just how much hair grease to use and how long to keep the stocking cap on to get the right kind of waves, and things like that.

I always felt that when he was watching me doing something, I would probably get it pretty much right. But I still wished he had gotten something to play with. I just felt he deserved something on a special day like Christmas. And I couldn't imagine that he had asked Santa for a sweater! Come to think of it, I guess he didn't go to South Center with us that year. So maybe Santa didn't know what he wanted, and just brought him the sweater.

Finally, I turned to the next picture with all the trees and grass. I hesitated a few moments. How could I get through that picture with all those trees and grass, and by that time I had only a little nub of a green crayon left. I really wished Santa Claus had heard me right and not slipped up. I was sure I told him I wanted a sixteen crayon box. He just should have stocked up with enough of crayon boxes that size.

I guess I must have looked a little puzzled and maybe even a little sad as I studied the picture and the few crayons left. My brother leaned forward and whispered to me in order to not to wake our Mother, so she could get her rest and get well soon. He said, softly, "You can use yellow for leaves."

A little later we tip-toed off to bed and I ended a very busy, happy Christmas day. I forgot about Santa's mistake and the dreary weather that day and how we didn't have turkey and a tree and things like that. I thought about my big brother lying next to me and how he really seemed to like his sweater after all. He kept

6

it on all day. At least I certainly hoped he did because, as I said, he didn't have a new toy or anything like that to play with all day long. But at least he seemed to like my coloring book even though it wasn't his exactly. I thought about that bright picture with all those autumn leaves on those trees.

Be Sure To Signal

There were times when my younger sister and I knew that something really special was about to happen in our house. Usually, it was associated with a visit from an aunt or uncle or cousin—someone special like that. You know, family visits, we liked that. It was different. It was a break in the monotony of things. I must have been around nine or ten when my first and most vivid memories occurred of these times. We were always busy doing something, just growing up I suppose. I am really sure our young lives were not what you would call boring or anything like that. It's just that there would be this close person, or a group in our house if for only a short time. As I said it might be our cousin, Doyle, who would come to "spend the night". Later, much later, I learned the phrase "sleep over", but we didn't use that term. Or it might be Aunty Mills coming all the way from Muskogee, Oklahoma. It really didn't matter. It was all special. We played outside more when my cousin came, baseball or hide-and-seek, and things like that.

At any rate, our Mother would clean the two-room kitchenette. I called it a house, but it really wasn't. But that's what we kids called where we lived, even if it wasn't exactly a house, and sometimes we'd just say "our place". But it was our home. The mirrors would be spotless; all the bed sheets on the roll-a-way bed and the pull-out couch would be ironed and folded. My job was to give the linoleum on the floors in the two rooms my best mop and wax jobs. On those occasions, I did not mind the chores.

Without question, I recall clearly, when our Uncle Dale, who drove a taxi at night in Detroit, and his wife Aunt Cora would visit it was special. I can't even say he was my favorite uncle. I guess Uncle Zeke, my mother's older brother, who lived in Chicago and sort of looked after us, was probably my favorite if I simply had to choose between them. Uncle Dale's and Aunt Cora's visits were very special. They didn't have children, and they gave special attention to us since our father and mother were not together. At least we felt they did. Uncle Dale seemed to feel that he should help our mother. Since he didn't have his own children, and his sister, our mother, was having a pretty rough time trying to raise three children in the middle of the Depression.

Uncle Dale was a tall, at least six feet, good-looking fellow, like all our mother's five brothers. It would not be exaggerating to say that my sister, my older brother and I fairly worshipped him. Always he seemed to wear a suit and a white shirt and a tie. He was always sort of quiet and had a slight smile on his face. We liked the way he would come and kiss our mother on the cheek and bend down and hug us—not big hugs or anything like that— but, you know, just "unclely" hugs. Aunt Cora would always say how we had grown. They would always ask us again how we liked school and just how old we were and be amazed that we were getting so big. In my case this was really not so true because I was definitely what you would call a "runt". We would grin and sort of stand to the side while they and mother talked. Every now and then Mother would ask us to get them a glass of water or more coffee or an ash tray for Uncle Dale's cigarette ashes or something like that. We would perform those requests like they were the most important requests in the world, and we were the only ones who could do them.

In the summers when they came, I knew this meant a trip to Comiskey Park with Uncle Dale to see the Chicago White Sox play, or to a Negro League All-star game to see Satchel Paige pitch. If anybody had told me that heaven was better than that, well ...I simply would not have believed them. I probably would have just tried to act cool, like Uncle Dale would. I wouldn't have said anything. That was something else I noticed about him, he didn't always have to say something, whether he agreed with you or not. Man, I really liked that. I thought that was really cool and smart to just keep quiet and sort of smile.

We loved that man!

We would go down to the Greyhound bus station, which was just a block from our house at 47th and South Parkway, and wait until the bus from Detroit came. Then we walk with them back to the house with an air of great pride and possession. We seemed, now that I think back, to act like we were showing them the way, as if they didn't know where our place was. And we would hope that our friends would see us strolling with our Uncle Dale and Aunt Cora. Later, after they had gone, we would tell our friends stories, completely false, of course, about how rich they were (after all, he did wear a suit, even when it wasn't Sunday) and how smart they were, and things like that. The veracity of the stories didn't matter. Uncle Dale was so special, he could make any story about him sound like it was true, even if it wasn't.

Mother would always fix a very special breakfast or lunch. When the meal was over, Mother, Uncle Dale and Aunt Cora would sit and talk. We liked that, too, because Mother always seemed especially happy when they or some of our other uncles and aunts came. She smiled a lot when they talked, and we liked that. It was clear to us that this was just one of those good times in our house. They talked about things going on with the other family members, and how things were going "on the job" with my uncle, family stuff, and when the last time they heard from so-and-so, and did another aunt or uncle ever get their teeth fixed, or get that roof fixed. Things like that. A few times I heard them talk about how bad "they treat our people" down home, and why so-and-so didn't just "leave that place and come up North". I remember one of Uncle Dale's favorite phrases, "At least up here, you got a chance to take a chance to be somebody". I never quite understood that, but I thought that was absolutely profound.

During school days I would go around repeating that sentence and trying to sound like Uncle Dale.

Uncle Dale and Aunt Cora never spent the night at our house, we didn't have the space anyway. But I remember distinctly my Mother reminding them every time they left in the evening to take the bus back to Detroit to let her know if they got home safely. My family always did that. It didn't matter whether it was back to Detroit or Oklahoma or Kansas City or even Los Angeles. They would telephone us and let the phone ring only once. Then they would wait about one minute, and ring again, and let the phone ring just twice. That was the signal. The family was in touch. That way we would know that they had arrived safely. This saved the price of a call, of course. You might call it "beating the system" or something like that. We would wait for those "calls" with all the intensity we could muster. We knew just about when they should get home, how long the trip took, how far their place was from the bus station, and things like that.

When the visits were over, we always felt a kind of sadness, but we also felt good. They had made a special thing out of our lives. They were family. No matter how soon after one of those visits when the welfare caseworker would be around asking about our missing father. No matter that the gangs in the neighborhood on South Side Chicago would be harassing me and stealing my lunch. No matter. Those things weren't special. Uncle Dale's and Aunt Cora's visits were special.

And every single time they visited and got ready to go, I remember the very last words my Mother would say, after the kisses and hugs, were "Be sure to signal".

Later in the evening the phone would ring once...and then twice. And we would just be quiet and smile.

Fight Night

I guess there was simply no way to describe it other than to call it a day and night of absolute contrasts. It was always the same. All day there would be a kind of tenseness, a sort of nervous beneath-the-surface feeling of excitement. People didn't talk about anything else but the event coming up that night. Joe Louis was defending his heavyweight title. Folks would ask things like, "Where are you going to listen? It was radio then, no television. Or "Do you want to come over to our place?" People would plan to meet at a certain place as soon as it was over, no matter what. I am not sure what "no matter what" meant. Of course, now I reflect, it obviously meant if he lost.

Anyway, if it was a school day, there simply was very little learning taking place. We were all too pent-up. At lunch time the guys would gather in the playground at Forestville School, 45th and Langley and just talk. We wouldn't play soft ball or anything. We would just talk about that fight coming up that evening.

Even the most confident and boastful among us would sort of lower their voices in a rather authoritative tone as if they knew just how "the Champ was going to take him." "Man he's gonna stalk that cat"; he's gonna feel him out, and stick-stab-and-jab him, and then, I'm telling you, he's gonna lower the hammer."

In a strange way the rest of us didn't argue with this observation and, I tell you, we always argued, certainly about sports. We just wanted it to be true that however he would win, just let him win. Then someone would assuredly predict just what round he would begin to "make his move". Now that I think about it, I absolutely do not recall anybody, and I mean the most argumentative guy among us, who dared to suggest that the Champ would likely not win. Nobody had that kind of courage. That cat would have been chased out of the playground.

Earlier in the week the boxing talk was mixed with ball playing, and guys even joked about how so-and-so—whoever that night's opponent would be—would be ducking and dodging blows and just praying to the Lord to spare him. Then someone would go into a mimicking, stalking, poker-faced dance with both hands held just like the real thing and whiff with a left, whack with a right cross, followed by a quick toe-tapping Bill Robinson type dance, which the real Champ never did, of course. He was too cool for all that strutting around. But all of this was earlier in the week, when we were more relaxed, and the big event was still several days away.

One of the great things about those times was you could always depend on some of the best barbershop talk you could ever get no matter what, just before and after the big fight. I guess it is pretty accurate to say that there was no other single event in our community during those times that so totally captured and focused our attention as the night of a Joe Louis fight.

Many of us followed baseball. I think the closest comparison to the excitement of a Joe Louis fight was a few years later in the 1940's when Jackie Robinson joined the Brooklyn Dodgers and came to play against the Cubs in Wrigley Field. All of my buddies became instant New Yorkers—Brooklyn, that is. I distinctly remember hanging on to every pitch, every stolen base, but that's another story.

A Joe Louis championship fight was the closest you could come to a thoroughly all-consuming event that linked our community to the "outside" world. We knew that we were not the only ones interested in the outcome. And, just as important, we knew why—why some were pulling for him and some were pulling against him.

Our day was planned around that upcoming night. Dinner, dishes, homework, errands, chores all had to be out of the way by, I think, something like 8 o'clock in the evening. If folks were coming over, they had to get there at least a half-hour ahead of time, not only to get a seat, but also, to get all the greetings and small talk out of the way. We even set our little, one and only, small table radio up on the high chest, as if that made it easier to hear! Also so everyone could see it as they listened. That sort of made it seem a little closer.

When the hour arrived, the streets outside all over South Side of Chicago became absolutely, eerily still and quiet. No jitneys ran up and down South Park Boulevard, now, Dr. Martin Luther King Drive. The street we lived on at 4630 South Park was two doors from the Met movie theater and next to a Jewish Synagogue. Who in his right mind would be out then anyway? The streets were dark and empty, like during one of the air raid, blackout drills during the War. As the preliminary announcements and introductions took place, you could tell that folks, sometimes as many as ten or fifteen, grew a little nervous in our crowded combination living room/bedroom. It was really a kitchenette, not an "apartment". Nobody joked now. The grown-ups hunched forward. Some squinting their eyes like they were thinking about what last minute advice they could give "Joe". Some just stared at the radio as if they were praying— remember it was always higher up on a chest. Everybody had done what they had to do, like go to the communal bathroom down the hall or get more water. No snacks, etc. were served...couldn't afford that. In our place snacks and refreshments came much later when television started.

Then, the bell for the first round!

Every single word that announcer spoke, we heard and instantly interpreted, and leaned forward for more.

"A sharp jab to the mid-section."
"A light blow partially blocked."

"And Louis is looking for that opening, now."

We hung; we waited. Some flinched visibly and frowned when the announcer's voice brought painful news, like, "He caught Louis with a good right. The Champ seems hurt. He seems stunned. He's holding on."

At that precise moment anyone in our little group in that cramped room would have leaped miles into that ring and taken the next blow for our Champ. Just to give him a few seconds to clear his head, to recover, to get himself together. We held our breaths.

The bell would ring, and we'd all just sit back a little...relieved for the moment. Not any chatter or small talk, just subdued and waiting. Having become used to many early-round knockouts by "Joe", we would begin to fidget. Maybe this particular opponent was not afraid of "Joe"; maybe "Joe" was confused a little by his opponent's constant dancing (we call it "running away scared"). Whatever it was, this fight was going on too long.

The bell would ring for the next round. There was no changed expression on "Joe's face", and the same steady, plodding stalking. That's good; he has recovered from the last round. Then, a long-waited comment from the announcer, "Louis put together two punishing combinations. Louis is moving in. The challenger seems to sense..."

Our crowded room got ready. A little air came from held breaths. Fists clinched and unclenched and even lashed out in sympathetic pantomime. Grunts of approval and encouragement could be heard. Smiles appeared. People sat up, ready, waiting. Lord, please let it be now.

The announcer continued, "And Louis follows with a good right to the head. Louis is measuring him; he's got him in a corner".

We couldn't hold it any longer. After all week, after a terribly tense day, this was it. This had to be it. People were on their feet, following every word, swaying with the descriptive account, now, openly shadow boxing. Some becoming more vocal, shouting, "Come on Joe, come on Man." Someone would quickly turn up the volume on the radio. The announcer's voice would be booming into the room, and we could hear the same voice coming out of other kitchenettes down the hall. The emotions were building.

The announcer in an excited voiced said, "Louis jabs with his left. A hard right hand finds it mark. Louis pushes him off. Louis feints with a left and lands a hard right upper cut. He's down. He's down." And those magical words, "Louis moves to a neutral corner….and waits."

But in our little room, we couldn't wait. We virtually exploded. Some people jumped to the radio, and tried to hush the others… picked up the count. "…3…4…5…" People started yelling and crying and hugging and joining in the count… 6…7…8.

The announcer again shouted, "He's up, he's shaking his head. He's up…. "The referee cleans his gloves and waves the fight on. Louis is moving in for the finish…another left, a right…another… He's down again."

The announcer told us the obvious, "The referee counted to 10. The handlers are in the ring, and…"

We started yelling again. We were finally liberated from the days of tension and apprehension. We had heard the announcer say those beautiful words we had heard so many times before: "And still Heavy Weight Champeeeonnn of the World…Joe Louis."

The night lit up. Cars came on the street honking horns. New Year's Eve horns blew. It would go on and on. 47th Street was alive and noisy and happy for hours. But some of us always waited before we went to join the fun. We wanted to hear the interview with our Champ. Sure, we could read about it the next day. We could see it in the Pathe News next week at the movies. But we wanted to hear it, too, live, as the saying goes now. We knew what was coming.

"Well, Joe," the announcer would start. "Congratulations. You fought like you said you would. You took your time. He couldn't hide. What do you have to say?"

And we all hushed and grinned and listened, knowing full well what was coming from that Alabama-born, Detroit-bred voice...coming across on the radio and across the many years of everything negative, over which he represented victory in our behalf. We knew.

"...just another lucky night."

We would go crazy all over again, slap our knees and each other's backs (the high five wasn't in yet), and yell some more. Then we go and join the celebration in the street.

"Let's Summarize What You Read": A Teacher's Personal Attention

She was my Sixth Grade teacher at Forestville School. Her name was Ms. Turner. I had several good teachers before, but I especially remember Ms. Turner.

Now, it is important to say without boasting or anything like that I along with a handful of others (there were thirty one children in the class) were looked upon as "pretty smart". We won all the spelling bees and things like that. I could always be the one who could be certain to get the correct names of the capitals of the forty-eight states. I could get all the lakes and rivers in the right places and stuff like that. Anyway, I sort of really liked school, especially, recess and the games at lunch. Of course, I was never scolded for being a "cut-up". Not a "goody-two shoes", but never in trouble where my mother had to come up to school.

Now, we knew Ms. Turner had her "favorites" — all the teachers did. These were the ones who led the line out for fire drills, and things like that. They would take notes to the other teachers in other classroom or to the principal's office. These favorites were the ones who were never told to be quiet in the hall.

So it was a big surprise one day when Ms. Turner gave me a note to take home to my mother. That never happened to me before. It surely meant something bad, very bad. The rest of the class knew it. I spent the rest of the day in total fear. Some looked at me in surprise and whispered, "Oh boy, you're going to get it now" or "What did you do?"

I was in panic. I took the sealed note home, gave it to my mother and stood in front of her and waited. She opened it, read it, folded it up, put it in her apron pocket and went on with her cleaning. After dinner I did my chores, washed the dishes and started on my homework. Later that evening just before bedtime my mother came into my little area where I slept on a roll-a-way in the kitchen, she softly said to me, "I am coming up to see Ms. Turner in the morning." Nothing more. I froze. Why, I could not ask. She would have told me why if she wanted to. I left for school and told Ms. Turner what Mother said. She simply said "Thank you."

Every single one of my classmates knew about the note and that my mother would visit that day. "What have you done?" "You're in trouble now!" "Man, I could not want to be in your shoes."

At the appointed time my mother came and she and Ms. Turner stood in the hallway for what seemed like an eternity and talked. Mother left and Ms. Turner came back into the room. She resumed teaching. Nothing more was said. Somehow, I'm not quite sure just how I made it through the day and to home. There, my usual routine, wash up, dinner, homework. Later that evening my mother said to me, "Ms. Turner will be coming to see you Saturday morning after breakfast for about an hour. So get your chores done fast."

That Saturday Ms. Turner came to our kitchenette at 4630 South Park Blvd. She and I would read a book and after a few pages she'd say, "Let's summarize what you read." Then I would talk about what I had read, and we would proceed. Sometimes the reading would be a long paragraph, other times several pages. I was never rushed, just read and summarize, read and summarize.

I do remember getting on the nerves of my older brother by five years and many of my playmates to whom I would often spout out, "Now let's summarize what you just said." I later discovered not only a new word, "summarize", but also that I had a reading problem. I could read, but I did not understand what I was reading.

Ms. Turner came to my house every Saturday morning for many weeks. Later I thought perhaps for three months. A couple of times we agreed to meet at the Hall Branch Library at 48th and Michigan. Most times at home when we finished, she would visit over coffee with my mother.

Literally, more than twenty years later after college and law school, I thought about what Ms. Turner, my sixth grade teacher at Forestville, had done. She had no grant, no stipend, she took her own time to teach me how to read more effectively.

By then I was a big-time university professor at Columbia University in New York City. I came back to Chicago to visit and decided to look up Ms. Turner. The Board of Education told me she had retired a few years earlier. After other efforts to locate her, I learned she had died two years before I found her location. I never got the chance to simply say to her, "Thank you very much".

I have had several good teachers in my life. Ms. Turner is the top of that list.

"Tell' em. . . So They'll Know:"
The Barber in Chair Number 3

I am sure some of us, my friends and I, chose barbershops not on the basis of the high skill of the barbers although that was important, but it was also on the "talk" that went on. I might call it ambiance or atmosphere now, but then we called it "talk'. Some shops were real talking shops. Where you could go at absolutely any time and hear two, three or maybe even four guys going at it for as long as two hours or more straight. It was about women, baseball, not as much about football or basketball back then in the late '40's because Black players did not play with the professional teams. Maybe there might be some really technical talk about card playing. I remember especially poker and bid whist, of course never bridge.

But those "talks" were always funny to hear; half the time someone would be shouting from one end of the narrow shop to the other. Sometimes, not too often enough for me, a really serious point would be discussed. I mean a topic where it really made a difference who was right and who was wrong. Maybe something like whether asafetida bags really helped ward off colds; my mother believed so; or whether it took longer to get downtown by taking the Number Three South Park bus from 47th Street or taking the street car to the "L" and transferring. I had a kind of vested interest in those discussions, and I frequently wished that some reasonably solid conclusion would be reached.

Most of the time you really didn't care who was right or wrong. Anyway, I had my own opinion on some of the topics like whether

Josh Gibson was more valuable to the Homestead Grays than Buck Leonard. But the grown-ups were doing the talking, and so, we just listened and saved our opinions for the backyard or the school yard. The barbershop was where we young ones saw the older men in action, equal to each other, no bowing or taking low, talking right up, making points, debating, and building egos. Sometimes cracking some of the best impromptu jokes and one liners you would ever hear. I remember hearing for the first time the sentence, "As busy as a one-legged man in a butt-kicking contest." Not original, of course, but I heard it first in one of those talks.

One shop was especially good for some Saturday "talk". Several of us, especially if it was raining and we couldn't play outside, used to meet there for our bi-weekly haircuts and just sit and savor. We would sit for hours, taking up seats because we could say that we were waiting for each other. And when an especially forceful point was made, the older guys would slap their knees or laugh, and we young ones would smile and wink. The younger ones didn't even laugh out loud too much, now that I think about it. I guess we just wanted to hear and not be seen because we sort of felt like this was really grown-up's business. The loser of that point wouldn't give up, he would just regroup and come back stronger, looking for a nod of agreement or a slight gesture of support from any one of the several barbers or the customers, one would be enough.

After a couple of months I began to pay attention to the barbershop "talk" more closely, not the substance, but, I guess what I now would call the "dynamics". I used to wonder how guys could argue literally for hours on end and never seem to care about the outcome. I mean seldom was there a real, final winner. You just made points all day long. I began to understand and like that. It is as if the game was never really over; the important thing was the playing. Much later, a lot of my interpretation came years afterwards, I thought of this as part of what is called the "oral tradition".

Then I began to notice something else. A couple of the barbers had their favorite "talking" customers who would come in and engage them on anything it seemed. This was always good for at least two hours of entertainment. I remember that a frequent discussion was which city, northern, of course, was better for "our people". Evidence ranged all the way from personal experience to what a cousin or friend had told about the place. One talker always made a strong pitch for Pittsburgh, I recall. I made a note to try to visit Pittsburgh when I grew up, just on the basis of that barbershop talk. Some of the criteria included such things as how a fellow could always "get work" in such-and-such town or "get on" at such-and-such plant, and so forth. Or it might include things like how "they treat you like a human being", and how "you can practically go anywhere there".

And then I began to see that different people played different roles. One barber might be a "starter". He would get something going between two others and then bow out and enjoy the show. Another, perhaps even a customer, would always take the opposite side, no matter what. I remember even then that that person always seemed less sincere than some of the other participants. This was disappointing because, although the whole business was one big Saturday afternoon show, I nonetheless did not want anyone to abuse it by being "insincere". We knew about the "put-on", but you left that on the corner or in the pool hall. Here, in the barbershop, you were supposed to mean it. This was fun, but it wasn't play.

At any rate, I soon began to notice the barber in the third chair, I think there were five or six chairs altogether. He never engaged in the talks. He never started one. He never laughed when the others did. Yet I noticed frequently that the very active talkers would make their comments in his direction. The shop could be filled with customers, everyone listening, laughing, slapping knees, nodding agreement, and just enjoying the talk. But the talkers would lean in Chair Three's direction. And if a talker was also a walker, he would be sure to walk close to or in front of Chair Three and make his points.

Now I should add also that there were some comments or remarks or specific sentences that could guarantee ending the discussion. Such as, "Put your money where your mouth is", which, of course, was an initial offer to make a bet. Sometimes, though rarely, a bet would materialize out of the discussion, but everyone knew that really wasn't the purpose of the talk that is, to prove something definite by betting and winning money. Anyway, some of the best talks couldn't really be bet on like Josh Gibson vs. Buck Leonard.

Another stopper, I came to notice, was, "Oh, man, you're just crazy. You won't listen to reason". This meant, of course, that the talker had run out of points to make, and he was now signaling that he was pulling out, not losing, by no means. Perhaps someone else could get some other topic going.

I understood these kinds of code phrases, and they made sense. As I thought about it later, I guess the only other way to end those sessions was simply to get tired, say so, and leave. On Saturday afternoon, most of those fellows could stay until closing time, which was about 5 or 6 p.m. But I guess that would've been a sort of insult. In fact, I know it. No matter how much you disagreed with your opponent, one thing you never did was to suggest boredom or disinterest in the subject. One might have another appointment, maybe, but unlikely, as everyone knew. They might have other errands or something, not "appointments" and even these probably not on Saturday Afternoon.

But there was Chair Number Three. I became fascinated with his role. I really don't remember his name. Most of the time they were all called by their first names by the grown-ups. He was not the owner of the shop. We knew that. The owner was always in the first chair up front, or in the last chair at the rear. He was not the oldest, which might have given him some claim to deference. He was really about the same age, or looked it, as the others. I am not sure if he had been there longer than the others, which might have given him some standing. I don't recall that he was considered a better barber, as such, than the others. Sometimes a barber had a particular reputation for doing something or other better than all the others which made him stand out a little bit. Like one guy could trim mustaches better than the others. Another could really do "conks", which were beginning to become fashionable. One barber was really good at using the scissors and comb for the trim-up. He was rhythmic. He would keep the scissors snipping all the time with a beat even when he was not actually using them over the comb. If there was a song on the juke box, he could snip in beat with the song.

But as I said, I am not sure that the barber in Chair Number Three had any particular reputation like that. I began to watch him more closely as the talks proceeded. The talkers didn't always cater to him, and I wish I had made a note at the time whether it depended on the topic. But when they did and when he responded, it was poetry.

If he responded in a certain way, the opponent invariably began to seek face-saving ways out of the Talk. That was about as close as you would come to a win/lose situation. That response from the barber in Chair Number Three was enough to put the stamp of "authority", yes, even call it victory for the one who successfully appealed to the "Chair". The response, if it came, was always the same. And it meant, I agree with you, or you're right, or you've got the better points, or something like that.

That was certain. We all knew that. It was just understood in the shop. Nobody turned on Chair Number Three and debated him. Nobody questioned him, because, frankly, he never said anything you could really argue with or question. If you made a real clear appeal to Chair Three and he just kept cutting hair, like he wasn't involved in the talk at all, and he made no response, then you had better look out because your opponent was sure going to make his move on Chair Three pretty soon.

I remember some talks going all afternoon on a Saturday at least for three hours. I had to tell my Mother that the shop was crowded and I had to wait. Finally a talker would make his move on Chair Three. He built his points slowly, and then, getting louder and louder and sometimes moving right in front of Chair Number Three. He would spin on his heels and, daringly, put the appeal directly. It would be something like, "Ain't that right?" or "Am I speaking the truth or am I not?" or some such.

One thing was sure, the appeal had to be clear, direct, and unambiguous. The talk had to have been going on for a while with pretty much all of the points on each side having been made. You shouldn't appeal to Chair Three too soon.

This must have happened at least two dozen times that I specifically remember. That barber in Chair Number Three, I thought, had something they all respected. Whatever it was, he had it, and he just spoke, throwing his weight to one side or the other. Not saying "yes" or getting involved and making points himself or countering any points made. Not saying "no" and embarrassing the talker who appealed to him. He just kept on cutting hair, checking in the back wall mirror to see how it looked, turning the chair and brushing away the loose hair without missing a snip of the scissors or without raising the clippers or, if shaving a customer without lifting the razor, and he would not look up.

For a double-split second the whole shop just waited. If he responded, all I ever heard him say in those talks was simply: "Tell 'em . . . so they'll know." Softly and rhythmically.

The whole shop relaxed. Nobody laughed and applauded or slapped knees or anything like that. But we all knew the verdict, to the extent that there could be one, was in. After that, folks just sort of began drifting out and saying so-long and see you next week. Somebody would probably put a nickel in the juke box. Probably put on Nat King Cole or the Ink Spots or Billy Eckstein.

"Best in the West – But Worst in the First"

Comiskey Park was the name of the place where Chicago White
Sox played baseball at 35th and Shields. I was an avid fan long
before I saw the stadium. Bob Nelson's radio broadcasts told me all
I knew about Luke Appling, Ted Lyons, Mike Kreevich and others.
The first time I saw a game there in person was in the late 1930's
when my mother took me one Ladies' Day to see my team play the
hated and feared New York Yankees. We sat in right field, and a
miracle of sorts happened that afternoon, the White Sox won 4 to 1.
I could think of no better way to inaugurate my first visit to that
shrine. I am sure I just grinned and giggled all the way home on
the Wentworth and 47th Street big long red street cars. My
mother was happy too. She was spared my silent tears if the Sox
had lost.

Of course, those were lean years for the South Side home
team. Winning was not a popular practice, home or away.
The Cubs up at Wrigley Field on the North Side were a slightly
different story. With Gabby Hartnett, Stan Hack, Billy Herman
and a few other prominent names the Cubs occasionally won
a pennant or came close, I recall. But I lived on the South
Side, and my team was the White Sox. Therefore, in those
lean days we Sox fans savored victories, especially over the
Yankees.

Like many youngsters, of course, I had visions of being a baseball
player, preferably, a shortstop like Luke Appling. A little later I

would frequently hop on a street car and go over to Comiskey Park and hang around after the game to get the players' autographs when they came out of the locker room. I remember being thrilled to be able to recognize them in their street clothes. They looked just like their pictures in the newspaper, sliding into second base, stretching for a wide throw, or chasing a pop fly. I kept a picture scrap book for years.

Many of us youngsters would yell and stick pieces of paper at them as they walked to their cars. When one of them would take your piece of paper and hastily scribble his name, you just sort of smiled and felt like a million dollars. Later, we would jump around and compare successes. Who did you get? I got so and so, and so forth. Those were heady days and this was a perennially losing team. But no matter, it was major league ball and those guys were big time. They traveled on trains to different cities; they got their names and pictures in the papers. We assumed they made a lot of money, but I don't remember much of any talk about that.

When I was around eleven or twelve, my Mother would let me go alone. I would wait around until after the seventh inning when the guards would let people come in free. That was absolutely great. I usually dashed to a spot in the stands behind third base or along the left field line. Then I could be one of the first to get down to the corridor outside the Sox locker room and, hopefully, get autographs or to just see our idols. As I think about it, I seldom if ever hung around the locker room of the visiting team. I guess that would have been sort of disloyal, if not downright unpatriotic.

One summer I had a little job in a neighborhood grocery store, delivering groceries, sweeping up, plucking chickens, weighing vegetables, etc. One of the pleasures I was saving for was to treat myself to a Sunday double header at Comiskey Park. One game was a delight, but to see two for the price of one was something like a Saturday double movie feature plus five cartoons and two serials. Although I'm sure, a double-header Sox outing was more precious.

I had the Sunday picked out weeks ahead. I am not quite sure, but I think the Detroit Tigers were going to be in town with Hank Greenberg and Charley Gerhringer, but it could have been the Cleveland Indians with Lou Boudreau. At any rate I began to live for that day, literally. I knew where I wanted to sit; I knew what players' autographs I definitely wanted to get. Weeks before I carefully planned what time I would leave home – very early, of course, because you could see the teams warm up.

The anticipation was heightened by the fact that this was not not only my first double-header, but it was also the first full game I would be attending alone and paying to get in with my own money. The excitement was building up and it was almost too much to bear. The only problem, obviously, was possible rain. If the games had to be postponed because of rain, I probably would have sunk into deep depression for weeks. But I didn't dwell on the possible calamity.

I slept well the night before, but I'm not sure how. I got up very early, did a few chores around our kitchenette apartment and kept my eyes on the clock.

Finally, it was time to leave.

For what seemed like hours I kept patting the ticket and street car money in my pocket. Money I had earned and with which I was soon about to buy my first ticket to a major league baseball game—two games for the price of one!

Now, it is important to indicate that I was, like many I'm sure, more than slightly familiar with batting averages, weaknesses and strengths of teams and players, and those sorts of things. I even knew something about where many of the players were born and grew up. In addition, I styled myself as reasonably knowledgeable about other matters not directly related to the playing field, like what the best seats were for getting the most foul balls hit your way; for dashing to the locker room, for looking into the respective dugouts. Those sorts of things were a part of my knowledge base.

Of course, everyone knew about the sun field and shadows on the diamond, etc. Early in the afternoon, the sun, coming from the East and shining into the left side of the field, would drench the third base and left field side. It could be pretty bad if you didn't have sun glasses. You had to constantly shade your eyes.

As I left home, saying goodbye to my Mother and sister, I tried to assume an air of casualness. We called it being cool as if I did this sort of thing all the time. I sort of sauntered to the corner to catch the street car, trying to conceal my bubbling emotions. I concentrated on how I would tell the ticket agent at the ball park exactly where I wanted to sit. I knew from many past seventh inning experiences what sections were the best. In addition, if necessary and possible, what rows were the best. Some seats required you to look around a post to see the action on some parts of the field.

Importantly, not only was this my first game alone with my hard-earned money, but I was getting a grandstand seat, not one in the center field bleachers, which, of course, was cheaper (later I spent many an afternoon out there). This was, indeed, my personal summer treat.

I transferred street cars at 47th and Wentworth and finally reached 35th Street. On the three block walk to the ball park I carefully went over in my mind what I would request in the way of seating. I had a first choice, right down to the section and row, second choice, even a third, fourth and, heaven forbid, a fifth choice. Obviously, I knew what ticket windows to go to maximize getting my preferred selection.

The hawkers were out selling banners, score cards, peanuts, popcorn. My wealth did not permit me those luxuries. But no matter, I had made it!

People were flowing toward the ball park, talking and laughing. I had assumed it would be a big crowd. That was good because I wanted a lot of yelling and pulling for the White Sox.

I had decided that I wanted a seat in spite of the early sun along the third base line as close down behind the box seats and the home team dugout, as possible. Loyalty again, but also a good shot at catching foul balls. The sun would be hot early on, but no matter, I had a newspaper to shade my eyes.

When I got to the window, the clerk said, "What can I do for you?" I announced in my most rehearsed and, hopefully, casual voice, "Section something or other, row whatever." Then I tendered, "Got an aisle seat?" I hoped the agent thought I did this all the time because I was so precise. The ticket clerk flipped through his tickets and in a few seconds said, "You're in luck. How's this?" He showed me a ticket very much what I had requested. He smiled and said, "Best in the West."

I smiled, nodded, and tried to remain cool although the excitement now was about to burst inside me. I gave him my money and took the ticket, and just to sort of let him know that

I was a pro, I responded, "But worst in the first," referring to the hot sun I would have to put up with in the first game. We looked at each other for a brief second and he winked at me and grinned.

Man, get that! I had no idea whatsoever that I would have said that and make it rhyme too. I felt grown-up. I was sure the ticket agent got the meaning of my subtle response. He had winked. Heck, I felt sophisticated like I did this all the time.

I think I floated or at least strutted into the ball park. The White Sox split the double header, winning the second game. I got three autographs and came home and wrote up every inning almost play by play. I called my write-up, "Worst in the first", meaning the score of the first game. The sun was hot, but no problem at all. I didn't even notice it.

A Newsboy's First Publication

It was every Friday morning early; it was just before seven, people were going to work. You begin to hear the sing-song chant of the Southside Chicago newsboys hawking The Chicago Defender. It seemed so natural at the time. So expected. "Chicago-o-o-o Defen-n-n-n-der." "Stick your head out of the window, if you want your Defender."

We spread out from State Street to Cottage Grove, from 31st to 60th street.

Some fellows carried their papers in little red wagons, some in old baby buggies, others in makeshift knap sacks. Since I never had that many, a point on which I will elaborate in a moment, I just carried mine under my arm.

I was always impressed by some of the melodic cries and rhymes bellowing forth from those young, strong voices. Some of those guys were really good. They must have practiced a lot. You could tell. They would string out "Chicago" or "Defender" in endless ways, emphasizing usually the "...go..." or "...fen..." adding highs and lows and harmonies. Now we would call it improvising.

As the people spilled out of those tenements and apartments heading for the street cars, buses, and "el" trains, or, indeed, sticking their heads out of windows, we would peel off newspaper after newspaper for ten cents a copy. I say "we", but I never really sold that many. In fact, I can never remember actually selling more than eight on the street, which I considered an exceptionally good day.

I remember this weekly venture mostly taking place in the summer when school was out, but I am sure there were guys who did it all year round. This meant that they had to stop by 8:30AM or so in order to get to school by 9:00AM.

We started early. We would get over to Moon's place on Prairie Avenue, a little basement room in a house midway in the block between 46th and 47th street. Moon was older than most of us, probably in his twenties. I do not know where the name "Moon" came from. It was probably a nickname.

Fellows would be there at 5:00AM, crowding around the tiny entrance, not lining up, unfortunately. When Moon opened up, we would crowd in and start shouting out our orders to Moon behind the counter. "Hey, Moon, gimme twenty." "Gimme thirty." The more enterprising, and to me, astonishing would yell, "Hey, Moon, gimme fifty!" I always wondered how anybody could sell fifty newspapers. They must have had regular customers, or knew the best places to hawk their goods – or something. But fifty, or even thirty or twenty seemed like an awful lot of papers to sell in a day.

As we rushed into that basement with the smell of fresh printer's ink thick in the air, which I loved, you jostled for position and started shouting your order – "Hey, Moon…"

We bought the papers for six cents from Moon and sold them for ten cents – four cents profit per paper.

I had four regular customers: my Mother, my Uncle Zeke, Miss Beecham, and a neighbor in our tenement whose name I have forgotten. They were sure, safe sales. Then I would venture out and buy three or four or maybe even five more and hope like the dickens I could croon my way to enormous additional profits. It seldom happened. My Mother and older brother always encouraged me to do that, even advising where I might stake out an advantage in the neighborhood. Don't wait until the people get to the busy corners; get them in the middle of the block as they left their homes. This worked sometimes, but invariably I would set up at the corner of 47th and South Park, a half block from my house.

Only a few times, as I remember, did I get as many as three or four sales in rapid succession; this would be a really good morning. When this happened, I would have to go back and get my allotment for my regular customers. But I would have as much as twenty-four cents to twenty-eight cents profit. This was a good haul in those days of the 1940's. It was Saturday afternoon movie money at the Met which was five cents, plus enough for popcorn and candy. Wealth and enjoyment with a little left over.

Therefore, when I'd see those guys coming into Moon's and ordering thirty and forty papers every Friday, I just assumed that they really must have been pretty well off. They probably made enough to take the bus downtown and go to a movie in the Loop and more than just on Saturdays!

Once I vowed to myself all week that I would get to Moon's and order at least twenty! This meant a one dollar and twenty cents outlay, but it also meant eighty cent profit if I could sell them all.

I practiced my yell, improvising first on Chicago, then on Defender. I carefully plotted my route, not the beaten paths or crowded corners. I calculated the time when I thought most people would be going to work. I also knew that the best locations also meant the stiffest competition. The more potential customers there would be the more competing sellers.

All week I planned and cradled the hard-earned one dollar and twenty cents. As I edged my way to the counter at Moon's, listening to the din of confident shouts, "Hey, Moon, gimme twenty." "Moon, gimme thirty." I worked up my courage, but the best I ever managed was "Hey, Moon, gimme...." It was not until that exact moment that I chickened out "...gimme ten." A little better than six, but hardly twenty.

The Chicago Defender was a weekly institution in our community. It told about things we didn't read about all week in the daily papers or hear on the radio. It had lots of pictures of people we knew. It had twists on stories we heard discussed in the barbershops. It told us about Joe Louis and our favorite ball players, Satchel Paige, Josh Gibson, Buck Leonard. It had political news, especially about "down South" where things were "bad for our people". But, for me, above all, it had the Bud Billiken Page.

This was a page devoted to the young readers in the early teen age range. Bud Billiken was a fictional character sponsored by the newspaper. Youngsters would write to Bud Billiken, and sometimes the letters would be printed. There was an annual Bud Billiken Day Parade every summer which was a huge event. It would move up South Park and end in Washington Park. You could belong to the Bud Billiken Club by writing and getting a certificate or card. The page also printed poems and short essays written by young readers. I took the leap once and submitted a poem about "Cowboy Bill". You never knew, of course, if Bud Billiken would print your piece, but the excitement of anticipation was enormous.

Then it happened.

That Friday morning I went to Moon's. Guys were already there, shouting. A friend had gotten his twenty-five or so and was heading out. He called to me that my poem was in the paper! I froze and then rose it seemed like ten feet off the ground. The first thing I thought was how proud my Mother and my teacher, Miss Turner, would be. I had a poem in The Defender! We would send it to cousins in Oklahoma, Detroit, and Los Angeles. But that meant I had to buy more copies. The moment was exhilarating. I quickly glanced at my friend's copy, confirmed the publication, and plunged into the crowd at Moon's "Hey, Moon..."

I had enough money to get at least fifteen papers, maybe a few more. I was certainly going to get at least five more to send to relatives. That meant buying at least eleven or twelve. Maybe

I could even improvise on my hawking, something like, "Read all about it, read the greatest poem you ever will, read all about Cowboy Bill." I smiled to myself.

As I inched closer to the counter, my spirits soared. "Hey, Moon…" they shouted. I made it up front, leaned over the counter and started yelling out my order. "Hey, Moon…gimme…" At first I yelled ten. Then I yelled twelve. He hadn't turned in my direction yet. The thought of my poem in the pages of this paper made me want to tell all of them that they were selling my creative talents! They wouldn't have cared, or course, but no matter.

"Hey, Moon," I yelled. Moon kept grabbing papers, counting out orders, taking payments, and turning to the next shouter. I don't think Moon had a system, and to my knowledge no one suggested that we line up in orderly fashion. He just took whoever came within his vision and sound. "Hey, Moon…" I shouted. He looked at me.....panic. I knew I had at most two seconds. Moon didn't tarry. You shouted; he counted. I thought of my poem, about my first publication, about showing it off. I didn't think about the best routes to take to see that morning, or about practicing my hawking. But I knew, without thinking, that if I went too much over ten or so, I'd better get out there and hustle. Then I came back to my poem. This newspaper had my poem in it. I had been published. What the heck.

I shouted: "Hey, Moon…gimme twenty."

Our Sunday Morning Strategy

At first it was "The little red church by the library". Some years later after the war with a remodeling and substantial physical and membership growth, it called itself "The friendly church by the library". The library was the George Cleveland Hall Branch at 48th and Michigan. The church was Greater St. John Baptist. Years later the name was shortened to St. John Baptist Church. We had a small but regular Junior Sunday School class.

We met every Sunday at 9:30AM along with other separate classes, namely, older brothers and sisters in their own classes, and adults in theirs. We had our Sunday School lessons. I remember the classes had Sunday School cards with a religious picture on one side, there was a short scripture at the top on the other side, followed by a paragraph or two of interpretation. Then the teacher would lead us through a discussion of the meaning of the lesson and its relationship to our daily lives. Usually something like "Do unto others as you would have them do unto you," or "Honor thy father and mother."

These were pleasant sessions as I recalled them. They weren't really like real school in that the teacher really didn't "call on you" to answer some hard question or other. Therefore you didn't have to "study" or do homework.

It's also fair to say that one of the main attractions of Sunday School was getting together with my buddies afterwards. We would get out at 10:30AM, dash to the corner drug store at 47th across from the Rosenwald Apartments, buy candy, and stroll back in time for the 11:00AM church service. There we would be joined by our parents, of course, and the two church choirs would march in singing. There was the larger Senior Choir. It sang complicated, melodic hymns. There was the smaller but decidedly more swinging Gospel Choir. When they sang, you couldn't sit still. People clapped in unison, swayed, sometimes shouted. Of course, there was Reverend Johnson's preaching. He was good. He was tall. He had a flowing black robe. He spoke in a clear, deep, strong voice. He repeated himself for emphasis. He cajoled. He teased. He pranced around the pulpit. You could always follow his points. He had this habit of asking, "Have I Got a Witness?" when he wanted the folks to hear him good or to express agreement. The people would always respond with something like, "Go 'head on," or "Well, alright," or "Help him Lord," or "Take your time," or some such expression.

Sometimes Reverend Johnson would get going and you could just see and feel the people getting worked up. There were regular ones who would literally jump from their seats and shout with joy. We came to know them as, "Happy." They would leap up, yell, and just sometimes fling their arms about. Men ushers and lady matrons, stationed throughout the church would have to come down the aisle and gently restrain them. They would fan them until they cooled down. The service was never interrupted. Indeed, this was an integral part of the service.

Some churches on the South Side were known as quieter places, where the most people did was hum or sing softly. Greater St. John was a "shouting church". "Nothing wrong with that," one of the deacons used to say. "Let the Lord know you're happy to be in His house." Man, were some of those people happy!

Now, it is true to say that at times you could measure the quality of a sermon or a rendered song by the number of shouters it brought out of their seats. At the end of the service when the Reverend Johnson would "open the doors of the church", invariably there would be several new people coming down to join our church to become members. Reverend Johnson was good. The choirs were good. Our little church steadily grew and we always felt good on Sunday morning in that place.

It was also true that some of us youngsters were actually terrified at the prospect of being next to or near a shouter. We certainly weren't big enough to constrain those adults. Sometimes, when there were several shouting at once, there were not enough ushers or matrons to handle the situation. This was one reason I was always glad to sit next to my mother, even if it meant I couldn't sit with my buddies. My mother never shouted. She would tear up sometimes, but she never shouted.

At any rate, my one constant Sunday School buddy, Sam Cunningham, and I spent more than a few post Sunday School classes discussing this situation. Where we should sit. How to keep away from the sure shouters. We wanted to go to church. We actually looked forward to the music and to Reverend Johnson's preaching although sometimes he could go on for over an hour! But sometimes when our parents didn't attend, or we didn't sit near them, we came awfully close to being near a shouter. And to tell the truth that was terrifying. We knew they were "happy", but we also knew they were flinging their arms! Now, it was clear that we pretty much knew the "regular shouters." But occasionally you could be caught by surprise. Someone you hadn't expected to shout. Or just a particularly moving moment and it seemed that the whole place was erupting all over.

We were genuinely perplexed. We knew we had to do something because the previous Sunday a rather large woman, Miss Rufus, leaped out of her seat just three or four persons away from us that was too close. Then Sam and I hit upon an idea. We took our idea to a few of our buddies, as I recall something like six or seven. We decided the best way to handle this was to ask the deacons if we could reserve spaces on the front row with them, sort of permanent special seats. We didn't tell them the real motivation, of course. It looked like we were being especially religious or something, and the deacons and our parents loved the idea. Of course, Reverend Johnson was enthralled. He even made a point to weave it into a sermon, something about "Raise them right and they'll go right", or something like that.

Sam and I felt good. We got credit for doing something that really pleased the whole church. We were singled out, down front where we could be noticed. But also, we knew, where we could be "protected."

One Sunday soon after we dashed back from the corner drug store, savoring the penny candy we had bought. We entered the church and made our way to our special reserve seats down front. Church was especially crowded that morning. It must have been a special day. Like Easter, or Mother's Day, or something. I am not quite sure. We had by now a pretty good notion of who the shouters would be and where they sat. We had started a private little game among us of predicting who would shout and when. We had a sense of who would lead off; who would follow, and things like that. We even knew that when Reverend Johnson got to a particular part of his sermon and made a particularly emotional point there would be anticipated response. Sometimes he would shout himself, never out of control, but sometimes I think just to get it going. We loved it when he shouted, "Let me hear you say Amen!" or "Have I got a witness?"

On this particular Sunday, we could just feel the atmosphere. Reverend Johnson was ready. The choir was ready. The congregation was ready.

Sam, I and our little entourage marched down front. To tell the truth, we had begun to turn this entrance into a sort of show off ritual. We were real "Hams"! Approving sounds came from the church members, saying things like "Isn't that nice," and "So well behaved," and "Like marching for the Lord." We loved it. Ate it up. But we also knew we were marching to safety!

Service started. We were right. That place lit up almost from the start, even when one of the deacons gave a long stirring prayer. The Gospel Choir had never been better. Reverend Johnson got into his sermon. Sam and I had our eyes on Miss Rufus. This morning, it was not a matter of if, but when, and we only hoped the ushers could get to her in time, because the people next to her, to tell the truth, didn't look too strong.

Reverend Johnson was going. The church "talked back" with words like "Amen" and "Help him Lord" and "Go head on." I always liked to hear "Make it plain." He moved across the pulpit, back and forth. After almost what seemed like an hour he was winding down. The shouters were all over the place. The ushers and matrons were kept busy that morning, holding flaying arms, fanning, and dashing off to another.

Reverend Johnson was in and out of the pulpit. Then he was in front of us. He kept preaching, and he looked at us and sort of swirled and cried out, "Have I got a witness?" The church erupted again. Miss Rufus leaped out of her seat. Sam and I spied each other out of the corners of our teary eyes, and our lips curled slightly in little smiles. He strongly denied it later when I kidded him, but I distinctly heard Sam Cunningham softly, but fully moving his lips mumble under his breath, "Go head on."

Week-Long Movie Actors

It started first thing every Monday morning at school. And it would last virtually all week, tapering off a bit around Thursday and Friday.

We would come fresh from our Saturday at the local movies, and we went over every single aspect of each double feature film and each of the several serials. We repeated dialog almost verbatim in many cases, mimicked fight scenes, fell off imaginary horses the way Tom Mix and Hopalong Cassidy did. We hitched our belts and swaggered as we talked the way James Cagney and Humphrey Bogart did. We marveled at the way the hero in the serial was saved from the previous week's certain disaster. "Man, did you see that!" "Boy, that was cool."

No matter that it was also absolutely absurd, the serial would end the previous week with the horse and rider definitely going over the cliff. This week both seemed somehow to stumble just before the edge or be rescued in some miraculous way before the fatal plunge. The previous week's serial ending with a shot fired dead at the hero from short range would get transformed the following Saturday with the gun jamming or being shot out of the bad guy's hand or something like that. Who knows!

At any rate Monday morning came and the rehash was on. Sometimes, since we knew that the hero would survive what seemed like imminent death, we even speculated how he would be saved. Thus, in a sense, we participated in the game of trickery.

There was little to interpret. Nothing was subtle. It was action we wanted in our movies, and action we got. Talking scenes that were too long usually got drowned out with low but audible talk in the darkened theater. "Love" scenes might draw a whoop or whistle, but the movie makers and theater owners knew those were not what would bring us to spend our nickels and dimes. And so there were few of such scenes in the movies we saw on Saturday afternoon.

Some of the guys at school took to the Dead End Kids right away, and I think at least ten gangs must have been formed that week alone. Each giving its members names reasonably similar to those on the screen.

No doubt about it James Cagney was a clear favorite. George Raft was popular too, but he danced too much and didn't slug guys enough or get slugged. Bogart was probably the coolest, but I think there were several candidates over time for that title. You could tell about Cagney, though. During the War when the movie stars would come to town selling War Bonds, James Cagney drew the largest crowd by far when he attended a Bond Rally at 47th and South Park.

The weekly movie-going process was simple. About 12:30PM to 1:00PM every Saturday, the line would start forming outside the Metropolitan Theater on South Park. The movies started at 1:30PM. There were at least four cartoons, three serials, a Pathe News, and two full-length features. If we did not stay to see the films over again, which required parental permission, we would be out by 5:30PM. The cartoons and serials were shown only once in the afternoon.

Without question until the War began, the Pathe News was the least attractive feature of the afternoon. The News usually only showed men getting on or off trains, talking to reporters, and walking in and out of buildings with an announcer telling what was going on. Frequently, President Franklin Roosevelt was on, saying something from his desk. In the evenings when the adults were in the theater, there would be applause for him even before he said anything. Clearly, he was their hero. My buddies never questioned that, of course. We just assumed he deserved it. Sort of the way Tom Mix did.

It was also clear that the "Met" had the best popcorn of any theater on the South Side. Except for the Regal Theater across the street in the next block near the Savoy Ballroom which was more ritzy because the big bands played there along with films well into the fifties. Of course, you could always depend on a little argument on that point. Some guys even went so far as to suggest The Owl or The Public, clearly second-rate theaters in the neighborhood. But the popcorn aroma in the "Met" was fantastic. It oozed throughout the place. There was a rumor that the ushers got all the free popcorn they could eat, which meant, of course, that becoming an usher at the Met could easily have been the fulfillment of a lifelong career. Once some of us tried to figure out once what made it so good. Maybe it was the amount of butter or salt, something. Once a fellow in our class named John went to a movie downtown, and came back and reported that the Met's popcorn was even better than there. That did it. The Met's popcorn even sounded good, popping away in the lobby.

One particular Monday, I will never forget it, we had all just seen James Cagney in "The Roaring Twenties". At times I am not sure which was more exciting, seeing the actual movie on the screen, or rehashing it all week with my buddies at Forestville Elementary School. In any case, the two went together. Cagney was especially good in this movie, we all agreed. We went through the entire story, correcting each other's memories of exact lines, adding our own slight embellishments, cocking our guns behind imaginary parked cars, doing somersaults when hit, reveling when the bad guys got theirs.

John was especially good in reenacting scenes, but his Cagney imitation was generally recognized throughout the school as the best we had seen. No one could really come close to him. Too bad, we thought, that he probably couldn't be an actor. He would be great, but he couldn't sing or tap dance worth anything, so that was out.

It was also true that some of our reconstructed tussles would get out of hand at times and end up in a real honest-to-goodness fight between two or more. This did not happen often because we really were more interested in our week-long acting careers than in fighting each other. But this particular Monday there was excitement in the air. It started before the 9:00 o'clock bell. In fact some of us came a little earlier so we'd have longer. It continued at morning recess, and reached high fever pitch at lunch time. John as Cagney was in rare form. We all chimed in, adding our version of a particular scene. No one dared "do" Cagney, of course, but John. When "our movie" ended, we'd find some excuse to start over, usually with something like, "And do you remember when..." There were script writers all over the school yard. With a good one like The Roaring Twenties, we might not get to the other film or to the serials until well into the week.

At Monday lunch we were in the middle of a particular action scene. Some fellow acted out a part and slugged "Cagney" from behind. It was a forceful blow, too much so. He just got carried away with himself. There was a brief pause as John lurched to the ground, rolled over, shook off the blow, got up, dusted himself off, eyed his attacker, and we all knew that we had moved from Saturday to Monday. The bell rang, ending the lunch hour, but no one responded. John squared his body, put his best scowl on his face, hitched his belt, and in his best Cagney posture he snorted, "You --- dirty -rat." The play acting was on.

We were ten minutes late getting back to class. Our teacher was furious. We would have to stay after school as punishment. But "Cagney-John" had never been better. We all agreed to that as we turned to multiplication tables, spelling lists, and locating the corn belt states on the U.S. map.

"Just Stop Counting:"
Advice from a Revered Professor

I first met Professor John Hope Franklin when he had just been appointed to a position at Brooklyn College. I was on my first post, a position as an instructor at Rutgers University, Newark, New Jersey. His appointment was national news. There were very few "full" professors in colleges and universities then. His reputation was well-known. He had been offered several positions to head Southern Black colleges. He had turned them down. He wanted to be a "Professor."

I had read his classic history book, "From Slavery to Freedom". Interestingly, throughout my undergraduate, law school, and graduate studies, I never had a course that referenced his book. To be sure I majored in Political Science and minored in History. But no course I took had a reading list that included any reference to Professor Franklin's work.

This did not surprise me. I had gone to predominantly white colleges and universities in Chicago. I did read about "Black history" at the Hall Branch library on the South Side. I also listened to a lot of sidewalk "lectures" from speakers on 47th Street and at the Washington Park Forum, but not in my formal higher education. There were no Black study courses, as such. But the research and books and articles were there. In elementary school, we celebrated "Negro History Month."

During this period I had decided I would go into Law and, hopefully, someday become a "Professor of Law" at Howard

University. That was my goal. On my own I read the academic and literary work of dozens of Black scholars and writers.

These works made sense to me. They dealt with the slave trade, the struggle to end slavery, the Civil War, right up to and beyond the New Deal and World War II.

I read. Then I began wanting to be a "scholar"; frankly, the word used was "Professor". The subject intrigued me. I wanted to be a part of it somehow. Also I wanted to not only study it, but also I wanted to teach it. Soon it occurred to me that I also wanted to be a part of it – not just to tell about it, but to act in it. Soon, the phrase "academic/activist" appeared. But that seemed quite frankly too pretentious.

So when I met Professor Franklin in 1964, I had already taught in a few Black colleges in the South (Miles College in Alabama, Albany State in Georgia, Tuskegee University in Alabama). Dutifully I had written articles in Phylon, Journal of Negro History, Wisconsin Law Review and attended the Annual Convention of the American Political Science Association. No question, I insisted on being a "scholar" (academic) – whatever. I would not be satisfied simply publishing, getting tenure, and lecturing and grading blue books.

I wanted more.

I wanted my students not only to learn about government and politics; I wanted them to be engaged in the political system, to participate. I really believed there ought to be that connection.

On the scholar side I had more than a few informal chats with Professor Franklin, especially, after he came to the University of Chicago and I was teaching at my alma mater, Roosevelt University. I loved these few times together. We talked about many things. More than once, he insisted that I not call him "Dr. Franklin". If I had to acknowledge the age-difference between us, he preferred "Professor." I liked that.

Later, I became "Chuck" to him, and he "John Hope" for me.

He frequently talked about why he had not wanted to stop "professoring". He loved teaching. He said once, "I'm not much of a marcher, myself, but I will certainly teach why you ought to be one if you want to."

Likewise, he was intensely aware of the relatively low esteem the white academic world held for Afro-Americans. He told me and, subsequently, wrote in a book that the white academic world often assumed that "Afro-Americans could not really reach high scholarly levels of research and analysis." He said, "It is as if they thought we could not count from one to ten. And then we began counting just to prove we could." He then turned to me and said, "Do your work. Be a Scholar. Just Stop Counting."

"Son, Can't You Just Come Home and Get on at the P.O." A Mother's Concern

I had the job I sorely wanted. I had a B.A., an M.A. and a J.D. Law Degree and I wanted to be a professor in a Black college; all that was certain. Late in the year of 1950 things were beginning to work out. I taught first at Miles College in Alabama, Albany State in Georgia, finally my "dream job" at Tuskegee Institute (now University) in Macon County, Alabama. This was to be the place for me.

I immediately became involved with the local civil rights group, the Tuskegee Civic Association (TCA). The Alabama NAACP had been banned by the state. Alabama was ripe for change. The Montgomery Improvement Association, headed by Rev. M.L. King, Jr., was headquartered forty miles away in the state capitol. The TCA was challenging the gerrymandering of Blacks in Macon County. This led to the successful Supreme Court decision – Gomillion v. Lightfoot (1962).

There was no question; I belonged in this environment as a professor with eager black students and open racial issues to challenge. It honestly never occurred to me that I should be any other place at that time. I had a wife; my daughter was born on the campus at John Andrews Hospital. The school's history was an important factor; it was founded by Booker T. Washington in 1881 and made more famous by Dr. George Washington Carver's research. The city was the home of the Tuskegee Airmen of World War II. The place reeked with "Black History". I felt I would have a lifetime professorial career in this great school. I absolutely felt that such a place would welcome not only my obvious academic credentials, but also my strong penchant for civic engagement as well.

At the same time I believed that my encouraging my students in civic engagement would be not only understood, but welcomed.

I was naive in both instances.

There were local norms, covert and overt, among my academic colleagues that I did not quickly grasp. Of course we should teach our students about the Constitution, and civil rights, and history "from slavery to freedom". However, our function should be solely to teach these things.

My error was I wanted them to learn how to participate in the struggle. More often the struggle was called "the Movement". I urged them to write their Congress leaders, urging them to support or defeat certain bills. We drafted a bill, HR. 7957 and had it introduced by Congressman Adam Clayton Powell. We corresponded with lobbying groups located mostly in the north and west to support the bill. Responses they received were good material for teaching about politics. Most of my students had never thought of writing their Congressional Representative.

When southern college Black students began "sitting in" to protest segregated lunch counters, public libraries, parks, recreational sites, etc., the Tuskegee University students planned a march through the city square downtown. They got a permit which allowed them to march, but there was to be no blocking the sidewalk, stopping at traffic lights, no shouting or signs. All these were observed. At least two hundred and fifty students participated. I was designated by the students as Faculty Advisor.

Afterwards, the students held weekly meetings on campus, inviting speakers from Montgomery. On one occasion Martin Luther King, Jr. spoke!

Activities expanded. The sit-in movement was launched. A meeting was held in Raleigh, N.C. out of which was formed the Student Nonviolent Coordinating Committee (SNCC). I drove up to Raleigh with four of my Tuskegee students. These growing activities on southern college campuses are now matters of American history.

My involvement was minimal at Tuskegee, but enough apparently to have the administration issue a letter terminating my employment. This process began on January 1, 1960. I was fired on March 1, 1960. The local and national Black press announced, "Tuskegee Professor is Dismissed".

My wife and I packed the child and the baggage in a U-Haul and headed home to Chicago. My "glory goal" was over. I was very disappointed, angry, and worried for several reasons. As it turned out no other Black college would touch me, that was certain.

I called my mother in Chicago and my brother. Told them what had happened. My brother was his calm unjudging self; he said, "Be careful on the road." My mother who looked forward to seeing her new-born seven months old granddaughter simply said, "Son, can't you just come home and get on at the P.O.?"

I did. I worked the full midnight shift at the branch downtown in the Prudential Insurance Building on Wacker Drive.

"One Hamilton is Enough"

I was never really naïve about race relations and all the writings and discussions about America as a haven from Nazism. Of course, I was a patriotic advocate in World War II, Hitler, Mussolini, "those Japs"—were all bad people. The United States of America, in spite of lynchings, segregation, and "White Only" signs was still better.

Anyway, there was always hope "Up North." The Chicago Defender told us so. Plus, we, the young blacks born in the 1930's, really believed our parents and elders who constantly told us "Get your education". That was like "brush your teeth", "Take a bath every Saturday ", "Mind your parents", "Take your hat off in the house", and "Go to church on Sunday".

There were rules to obey, lines not to cross.

We, young Blacks, male and female, knew these rules. Some broke them; others abided by them. Consciously I decided to play by those rules and win. I decided to get as much education as I could and challenge the racism and obvious falsehoods of a segregated society.

I laughed along with elders at the jokes on Amos and Andy. But I still did not think them funny. That's why when Joe Louis won, and Jesse Owens won at the Olympics, and Jackie Robinson stole those bases, we slapped our knees and cheered so loudly.

In the 1950's, getting a B.A. degree, a law degree, an M.A. and in 1964 a Ph.D I knew I had done what the rules had required as far as "get your education" was concerned. Then in the mid 1960's opportunities opened up, teaching jobs at Rutgers University, at Lincoln University in Pennsylvania and back to my Alma Mater, Roosevelt University in Chicago. This latter position seemed ideal. I was "back home, Up North" and still remaining involved with civil rights activities.

In the meantime through my activities with the Student Non-violent Coordinating Committee (SNCC), I met Stokely Carmichael. In 1966 we agreed to write a book for Random House. Black Power was published in 1967. Carmichael became an international figure. The book took off. It was provocative. It was controversial. It scared some people, Black and white. It emboldened others. It confused many liberals, Black and white. Sales soared.

My wife and I almost paid off our mortgage in Evanston, Illinois.

A few years earlier I had been fired from Tuskegee University and had returned to Chicago to work at the Post Office. I could not get a teaching job at any southern Negro college. Roosevelt University hired me from Lincoln University. My visibility was high. After every summer riot in the country, I was on the list to be interviewed by the media.

They would ask:

Will there be another long hot summer this year?
Does "Black Power" mean violence?
Does "Black Power" mean separation?
Does "Black Power" mean "kicking whites out of the
civil rights movement?"

Government agencies and philanthropic organizations gave grants to all and sundry scholars and newly born sycophants. There developed a saying, "The revolution will not be televised." But I submit, it sure could be hustled. And it was.

Job offers to me that were few and far between only a decade earlier were now flowing in. I decided to stay at Roosevelt University until an "offer came from Columbia University that I and my wife could not refuse". We considered it carefully, and decided we had to take it. The amount of my salary and a few items like a "Chair" and research funds to be sure caught my attention.

I played it nonchalant until Columbia in effect said, "Look, we want you. Here's what else we'll do." They promised to give us a mortgage, pay the tuition of our two pre-college daughters and provide free tuition to my spouse. She already had an M.A.; the tuition was for her full attendance at Columbia's School of Social Work, one of the top schools in the country, through to complete her work on a doctorate degree.

Back in Evanston, my wife and I thought about this final offer for a full five seconds. That's how long it took for me to call and accept. Columbia said that they were very pleased. I was cool. I simply said: "We look forward to being there."

I informed Roosevelt University of my decision. I had already indicated to the administration my unease with its reluctance to hire more Black and liberal outspoken faculty. Staughton Lynd was the example I gave. I was also aware that a few trustees had voiced in writing to the President their displeasure at some of my writings.

Robert Runo was my teacher at Roosevelt in the 1940's, long-time colleague, and not one to hold his peace. He informed the University of my leaving. The Dean was upset with my reference to the Lynd affair. The Dean thought I was unfairly criticizing the University.

As was his wont, Runo responded to the Dean, "Chuck was in no way unfair in his remarks about tokenism."

He pointed out that several vaunted liberal professors had openly announced flatly and honestly that "the university could not afford another controversial person"; in other words, "One Hamilton is enough." Professor Runo continued, "I do not hesitate to assert that if the Hamilton – Carmichael book had come out six months earlier, our department never would have been permitted to hire Chuck."

This letter is in the files of my alma mater. It is also in my files and mind.

Three decades later the University gave me an Honorary Degree and I joined its Board of Trustees. Go figure!

"Just Have the Word 'Black' in it"

I was never really naïve about race relations in the United States both South and North. I knew what Professor Franklin had advised was sound advice. I knew what Professor Runo had told his colleagues was absolutely correct. But also I believed that the age-old "civil-rights movement" was "making progress."

I did not need to be reminded that "racism" came in many forms and in overt and covert methods. I was not fooled by those who saw interracial marriage laws declared unconstitutional as the end of racial bigotry. The same was true with restrictive covenants, ending segregation in the military, and countless other victories over "de jure" segregation.

I knew that the Black students Sit-In Protests in the southern states and other similar efforts earlier by CORE in the North were not delivering "the final blow" against "racism". But I did believe that such efforts and victories were part of a long continuous struggle for a "serious" democracy. The important thing was to maintain "the struggle."

At times I smiled when friend and foe reprimanded me for my "black power" positions. When the demand came from Black students for more courses on "Black Studies" and more employment of Black professors, I was quite aware of the political ramifications of those demands.

Colleges and universities around the country virtually rushed to hire Black teachers. In some instances the quest was couched in interesting language. "Diverse faculty sought" and "Equal Opportunity Position" were becoming popular and acceptable terms. All these developments led to a sense of progress. In fact "progress" was the important word that kept some of us going. We did not use "post racial" or "post bigotry" or some such language that indicated finality. And the frequent local events—race riots at beaches (North and South), stoning of homes of Blacks moving into an all-white neighborhood—were constant reminders to keep your guard up.

Thus, when some previously all-white schools, especially in the Ivy League, began recruiting more Black students and even professors, these efforts were indeed seen as progress. At the same time I was aware that these developments came from mainly Black students and activists in an on-going political struggle. Several of the colleges rushed to establish Black Study programs and courses. Black teachers especially were now sought, notwithstanding that their academic training might be in some field having nothing to with race or ethnicity. The important point was to have a Black presence.

I was approached by several schools. I finally chose Columbia University over Harvard, Yale, New York University. The choice was easy. The others wanted to start programs of the sort in Black Studies. I was interested in a position in a Political Science Department. Frankly, I felt many of the quickly established Black Studies programs would become academic Black ghettos on campus since they were simply to satisfy a crisis demand from students. I was joined in this view by a colleague at Columbia in the Anthropology Department, Ambassador Elliott Skinner.

I chose Columbia precisely because they made me an offer I could not refuse.

They gave me a Chair, teaching assistants, research funds, free tuition for my pre-college daughters, free tuition for my wife who already had a B.S., M.A. who planned to get a doctorate in Social Work which she did. No other offer came close.

We packed in a hurry.

Columbia asked what I wanted to teach. My first teaching job was at Miles College in Alabama. I taught five courses a semester. At Columbia ten years later I would teach two courses a quarter; there were three quarters. I indicated I definitely wanted to teach an undergraduate course "Introduction to American Government".

For my Graduate Seminar I indicated, "Political Modernization in Urban Politics". The concept of modernization was a popular political science term I borrowed from my Ph.D professor, David Apter, at the University of Chicago.

The Chairman of the Political Science Department at Columbia looked at me, arched his eyebrows and said, "How do you think you got here? I do not care what you teach. Whatever you teach, just have the word 'Black' in it."

We understood each other.

Saturday Night and Sunday Morning
in Apartheid Soweto

The story was in his eyes as he spoke the words. He was a twenty-five year old South African man, a journalist by profession, a warrior by necessity.

It was at a party somewhere in Soweto in January 1980. The people there were from two continents who had been brought together by history. Mandela was still in prison. And the music played.

But my friend (I assumed) told his story seated in a corner with his eyes. For fifteen months he had been detained by the authorities in solitary confinement. His crime? He shrugged and smiled. He had been protesting apartheid. His worry? At first his family! He told us his father was born in 1912 was getting on in years. His mother born in 1919 had to be cared for. So he worried. And there he sat detained by an evil in the land of his birth, by an evil that turned him into an enemy because he was Black and cared about the children, about his people about what he called justice.

We will give you time, lots of time, to think about your answers, boy, they told him. For months they left him alone with himself, with thoughts of his aging parents, with worries. Then the beatings started. But he told them he, too, would be violent! How? Only by crying! He would cry as they hit him because he felt pain, intense pain, nothing more. No guilt, no shame, no remorse, no confession. The liberals say there must be peaceful change, and we nod in sanctimonious agreement. So, he would fight them violently—his way, by crying. He screamed, he said when they beat him, but he decided to beat them, only by crying, by surviving and, never, he kept urging himself, never pleading for mercy.

Then he devised ways to live even as his body ached. He would take the three pieces of bread they gave him each week and with his spoon, no knife, of course, cut off the crust. With the pieces of bread he carefully made twenty four pieces and placed them on the squares of his wash cloth. And he played chess.

His left hand would be the authorities, the enemy; his right hand because he is right-handed would be the prisoner – himself. And if the left hand lost, he would be released soon; otherwise, he would lose and maybe never see his family again.

This incredible young man knew that first he had to be honest with himself. He had to give no favors to the right hand. So he divided his mind into two parts, one for the left hand, one for the right hand and he played. He played his chess game of strength and survival, of life and liberation.

The beatings continued. He would, at first, count the blows until they just blended together as one constant pounding, one undifferentiated pain. He would hold the walls for support as he made his way back to his cell, his home. Hurt, pained, but strangely proud. He survived. The words were not necessary. The story was there in his eyes. As those eyes spoke the struggle of his people in that strange, bitter land, one remembered the words of one authority, "Revenge and hatred will get the Black people nowhere."

My friend spoke about the games he played month after month. He told about the ant he enticed into his cell and trained, so he thought. He talked about the fly on the wall that became his friend. He would entreat the fly, "Oh please, don't go away, Mr. Fly. Stay awhile. Keep me company". He spoke about the chess game. He improvised a night club act. "Man, I would be the performer, the band, the audience. Did you like my songs, folks? Did you like that one? Ah-ha. Good, good."

They beat him month after month. They beat his body, but his spirit remained intact. They bashed his head; he protected his brains. He had to win; he had to live, to survive and to beat this cruel place. One knew all this.

The eyes. The eyes never really cried; they only shed tears. No matter. Eyes do that sometimes because and only because the body aches so much.

He moved away from the corner and danced for awhile. The body they could not break now moved smoothly to the tunes of a Xhosa click song. In one place he swayed smoothly, confidently.

He had told his story of sin versus survival, of masochism versus manhood, of degradation versus dignity. He had beaten them for now. The eyes told you so.

It was getting late in that house in Soweto. There were other meetings, other stories to hear, other things to learn, other shrugs and smiles. Saturday night in Soweto would soon become Sunday morning. There was a church service to attend in another part of that Black South African township. The people would come to church. The other people who knew the stories those Saturday night eyes told and knew them all too well.

I went. The sun was bright as if there had been no previous night of stories of evil, no eyes telling of pain and persistence. It would rain later, but now the church was filled. There were children; there were songs; there were visitors; there were grown people, escaping if only for a few hours.

I thought of those eyes. I thought of that chess board made of a wash cloth and bread crumbs.

I thought of that fly that stayed and kept him company, of that ant.

I thought of those eyes that told the story of the night-club act.

I thought of my friend who was Black and South African and twenty-five who worried about his parents even as he heard the authorities coming to get him to beat him again.

I thought of the price that bitter land surely would pay for the countless times it had made such people hurt.

So, we sat in the church and I listened to them pray.

"If They Are Civilized, They Will Seek Revenge. That's What Civilized People Do." Opinion of an Afrikaner's Judge

It was during an International Conference on Human Rights in January 1979. The gathering included scholars, political activists, journalists, jurists, lawyers, from Europe and America. The conference was held at the University of Cape Town, Law Facility.

Nelson Mandela and many of his comrades were in prison. There was a wide range of political ideological views invited as well as multiple ethnic and religious delegates and speakers. I was invited, notwithstanding my being a banned author and a decidedly open anti-apartheid proponent. I was granted a one week visa, after much delay. I went notwithstanding the advice not to do so from many of my civil rights colleagues. I had agreed to be one of four plenary speakers.

I chose as my lecture the role of the Federal Judiciary in the United States in dealing with the right to vote for Black Americans. The ultimate goal of such efforts was, and still is, universal adult suffrage.

My intent was, admittedly, to demonstrate my knowledge of the constitutional law on such matters in the United States. No advocacy, no proselytizing. This was, after all, a law school sponsored event. But it was also 1979 in South Africa that was in the throes of international pressure to end apartheid through sanctions, pressure from within, or "by any other means necessary". In such circumstances I could hardly expect my topic and presentation not to produce wide response. It did.

The local press said that I caused a sensation by calling for the universal franchise. Some delegates indicated that the right to vote was in fact not a human right at all. But they said the mixed marriage act was such a violation. Others said I was speaking about something that was simply not reasonable in the Republic of South Africa. After all, they argued, people have to eat and they must be concerned about such realities and not some abstract notion as universal adult suffrage. Fair enough. I had heard such arguments many times over the years in the United States. Thus, these responses did not phase me.

During the course of the several days following, I was approached by many delegates to simply discuss the subject. On one such occasion a highly respected Afrikaner judge made his way to me. There was a break in the session. He obviously wanted to speak to me alone. Steering others politely away, he made our way to an empty table for two. We sat. He puffed his pipe, staring directly into my eyes. "Very interesting presentation, Professor."

He tapped the ashes from his pipe into an ash tray. His eyes never left mine. He continued, "But I suspect you Americans have reached a stage that can never happen here in our Republic." He sipped his tea.

"You see, if one man, one vote ever came to South Africa, we Afrikaners would have to go into the laager. This would be necessary because our children and grandchildren would be condemned to death. The Blacks here would kill us because of what we have done to their children." He sipped more tea.

He kept his eyes on mine. He was not being rushed or alarmist. "For you see, Professor, if the Blacks are civilized, they will seek revenge." (Pause) "That's what civilized people do."

We saw each other the rest of the conference, nodded, but never spoke again. I saw him a decade later during the Presidency of Nelson Mandela. We never mentioned our brief 1979 contact.

I had long since decided that I could not accept his definition of a civilized human being. I had hoped one day I would be a part of proving him mistaken.

"Daddy, When I Leave the Administration, I Want South Africa to be a Part of My Future:" A Daughter's Telephone Call

The long struggle to end legal apartheid in South Africa was over. The country had released Nelson Mandela and his colleagues from twenty-seven years imprisonment. Several years of negotiating change and gaining universal adult suffrage had been achieved. An election was held. Mandela became that nation's first Black president on May 10, 1994.

I was not there. I had been to South Africa many times since 1979 in many capacities. I watched the 1994 proceedings on television. The world was watching.

The United States had its delegation at the Inaugural ceremony. The U.S. Secretary of Commerce, Ronald Brown, was part of that delegation, as was several members of his staff, including my daughter, Carol L. Hamilton, his Press Secretary.

Some people called it a miracle, others just cried, and cheered. The whole world watched.

We knew this was history. We did not think about all the past problems that despicable society created. We did not think about all the future problems it faced. We just knew that tomorrow would be the start of a new day.

It was a victory. It was not nirvana, but it was simply a "good thing."

Some people somewhere probably did not want it to happen. Some probably thought, "It couldn't work." But there were also ones who thought it could not happen in the first place.

That evening, my daughter called me from their hotel in Johannesburg. She had been in Pretoria at the inauguration soaking it all in. She knew of my many trips since 1979. She was exuberant.

"Daddy, you should be here."

I told her that she would be my representative from now on. I did not need to be there.

We talked on. She described the entire scene how she had felt meeting Fidel Castro and his entourage; talking to potential new members of Mandela's administration. She stated these are the people who "will be actually running this country".

I just listened. At one point I got in a word, "Are you taking notes?"

She paused, sighed and said, "Now, you know I am."
We laughed.

She talked on. I heard a new, different daughter; a new grown-up (she was thirty-seven); a person who was becoming more than "my little girl". I heard a person I no longer needed to worry about. I did not need to teach her how to drive a car; how to deal with aggressive personal advances. She was now literally "in the world".

Finally, after talking with her mother, she asked to say a few more things to me. I thought she wanted to talk a bit more about some of the people she had met and about a few I had met who wanted to tell me hello, that sort of thing. Not so.

I took the telephone and she did not say "goodbye" or "talk to you when I get back" or "tell so-and-so hello" (her usual sign-off). She paused and said, "Daddy, when I leave the Administration, I want South Africa to be a part of my future."

I said, "OK, Honey Bunny, I'll throw in with you."

Our daughter, Carol, came into her own. She would tell her parents, jokingly, "You two are academics, which is nice, but I am going into the real political world."

She did and ultimately became the Press Secretary for the U.S. Secretary of Commerce, Ronald Brown.

My wife and I would "concede" to her when she would return from one of her hundreds of trips overseas for the Department of Commerce. She would regale us with stories about the Shah of Iran, the IRA in Ireland, the leadership in Israel, and the important figures in the Republic of South Africa.

Carol matured in a way that made us both pleased and proud. One evening at dinner after she had returned home from one of her exciting encounters, I turned to her and said, "Honey Bunny, I guess you really need not to be a professor after all."

She looked at me and smiled slyly and said softly, "Thanks, Daddy. I'm so relieved."

Carol Hamilton

Dona and Carol Hamilton in 1982 at Dona's PhD graduation
ceremony.

Carol briefing Secretary of Commerce's staff 1996

"You Can Use Yellow for Leaves"

Odyssey of an African-American Professor

Photos

Dr. Charles V. Hamilton
Biography

Professor Charles V. Hamilton, retired Wallace S. Sayre Professor of Government and Political Science at Columbia University, is the author of several books, including *Adam Clayton Powell, Jr.: The Political Biography of an American Dilemma* and co-author with Kwame Toure' (Stokely Carmichael), of *Black Power: The Politics of Liberation in America*. He received his Ph.D from the University of Chicago and has taught at several universities, including Tuskegee in Alabama, Rutgers in New Jersey, Lincoln in Pennsylvania and Roosevelt in Chicago.

Professor Hamilton was one of the first Black political scientists to visit South Africa during the apartheid era in 1979. His travels to that garrison state left an indelible impression on him. He became a member of the Council on Foreign Relations and continued to pursue his interest in the political and economic development of the African continent. In 1997 Professor Hamilton retired from Columbia, and is still actively researching and writing. He now divides his time between Chicago and South Africa. Through his teaching, books, and speeches he has provided a platform from which to debate the great issues of the post-civil rights era. Whether broadening the discussion or challenging his colleagues regarding the direction of the struggle for equality, Professor Hamilton has generated some of the most thoughtful scholarship on the current issue of race and the development of political justice.

Family

My Mother, Viola Haynes Hamilton, and her sisters, Lula, Annie, Leola and Emma Lee gave me an early sense of the importance of maintaining contact and caring among a family that was spread around the country.

They were the ones who always remembered to "signal", who sent holiday cards and gifts and who offered to help "if you need us".

Uncle Zeke was always close at hand in Chicago. He was very supportive of my older brother, Owen and his wife, Elizabeth (Lil).

Lil died prematurely at the age of twenty-seven from a cerebral hemorrhage.

Viola Haynes Hamilton

Mother and aunts

Uncle Ezekiel

Owen's wedding party

Margaret and Dailey Cannon are the maternal great
grandparents of Hamilton.

School

These photographs document the results of my family's and teachers' advice to "Get your education". My determination to pursue their advice was arduous on each level of achievement. It was difficult, but it was always fun. It was accompanied by part time jobs in grocery stores, local factories and the United States Post Office.

That was the normal assumption and expectation— study and work.

Ms. Turner and her Fifth-Grade Class at Forestville School in 1939. Charles Hamilton is seated in the first row second from the left.

Englewood H.S. graduation photo 1946

University of Chicago graduation 1964

Academic Activist

In these pictures is represented the beginning of a lifetime career as an academic/activist, combining research and writing on political science that focused upon the developing civil rights movement.

The Student Non-Violent Coordinating Committee (SNCC) was one of the main subjects of my work which produced a book, *Black Power, The Politics of Liberation in America*, co-authored with Stokely Carmichael while I was a member of the faculty at Lincoln University.

The writing and the lectures on this book as well as my subsequent role as a consultant for the National Broadcasting System (NBC) competed with my academic obligations.

However, I learned that the activist role was for me a necessary part of my academic role. The former informed the latter.

I could not have had it any other way.

Black Power cover Carmichael & Hamilton 1967

The faculty house at Lincoln University, Pennsylvania where Stokely
Carmichael and Charles Hamilton wrote the book, Black Power
September 1966 to August 1967.

Dr. Hamilton is consulting with the producer of the NBC series, "Urban Crisis" along with Daniel P. Moynihan, who was a Harvard University professor in 1968. Moynihan became a U.S. Senator and represented the State of New York for twenty-four years.

Charles Hamilton is at reception 1972 with Lerone Bennett, a senior editor for Ebony Magazine and a Black history scholar.

Foreign Activism

My academic/activist role began to include an internal
itinerary and a lecture tour to China in 1987.

My wife, Dona, and I were sponsored by the U.S. State
Department for a five week tour of seventeen cities where
we lectured at universities for the most part.

Dr. Dona Hamilton lectured on social welfare policies in the
United States and I lectured on the civil rights movement.

Lecture tour in China with Dona Hamilton in 1987

Couple going to
church in Soweto

At Lincoln University house
with Professor Professor
Levi Nwachuku

Africa

My wife and I chose this school, Pabalelo, in the North West Province of South Africa, to establish a memorial fund for Carol on the advice of local educators and officials who were familiar with the needs of many such schools.

The proceeds were used for supplies, computers, basic materials and building renovations.

Donating funds in memory of Carol Hamilton

Scenes at Pabalelo School

Students in classroom at Pabalelo School

Archivists at University of the Western Cape

More scenes at Pabalelo School.

More scenes at Pabalelo School.

Numerous conferences have been attended by Dr. Hamilton over the years.

In May 2000 he was a panelist in the gathering called, "Beyond Racism- A Comparative Study of Three Countries: United States, Brazil and South Africa" The closing session was addressed by R.S.A. President, Nelson Mandela.

Conference in the Republic of South Africa, "Beyond Racism" in
May 2000.

Shared Interest, Inc. invests in southern Africa's future by guaranteeing commercial loans to low income communities and their own financial institutions to create businesses, jobs, affordable housing and services.

Shared Interest, Inc. takes a delegation of interested donors to southern Africa on a regular basis. This photo of delegates and members of the staff of Shared Interest, Inc. was taken in August 2016.

In May 2017 at a fundraising event for Shared Interest, Inc. in New York City called, "Conversation for Change" Dr. Hamilton is joined by actor/activist, Danny Glover and the former Mayor of New York, David Dinkins.

Chief Nkosi Mkwedini greets Dr. Hamilton

Lunch with delegates including Lee Daniels.

Brief respite with tour delegates.

DuSable Museum

The DuSable Museum of African American History was founded in 1961 by Dr. Margaret Goss Burroughs. It was moved to its present location in 1973.

This institution has provided a reading room for the Dr. Charles V. Hamilton and Dr. Dona C. Hamilton Research Institute. The Institute will serve as a locale for their extensive archival materials and artifacts. It will become a center for eductional seminars adding to the vast collection and wealth of programs at the DuSable Museum.

The DuSable Museum

The DuSable Museum staff

Epilogue

As I reflect on this odyssey of mine, I end with the softly spoken encouraging words which remain carved on my soul by my big brother. In his gentle, caring way he was telling me how to meet and deal with a seemingly dire condition; a condition that seemed unconquerable and overwhelming at that moment. A forest of trees I could not finish for lack of green crayons.

I appreciated his words at that moment. I don't think I really thanked him then. I was a seven year old with a major task at hand! But I understand and remember those words now in more broadly-faced context – eighty years later.

Whether this involves finally realizing the care and patience of a Miss Turner, teaching me how to read; dealing with uncomfortable racial attitudes and experiences as a young professor; savoring the community and confidence of young friends; even having empathy with my young Soweto friends.

I always remember my big brother's wise advice:
"You can use yellow for leaves"

"Before the internet and the making of present-day social media pundits, Dr. Charles Hamilton was the leading intellectual theorist on the concept of Black Power; he co-authored the book, Black Power, with Stokley Carmichael—a book still relevant today. In this memoir you will read about his experience as a respected scholar in South Africa prior to the dismantling of apartheid and the election of Nelson Mandela. His story is inspiring, uplifting and enlightening. It is an odyssey of a Black man from humble beginnings in Muskogee, Oklahoma and Chicago's Black South Side to becoming one of America's first rate African American scholar/ activist. Just read it—let him tell you his story."
Professor Dwight Murph, Department of Philosophy, John Jay College (CUNY).

"Dr. Charles Hamilton's rich experiences as teacher, scholar, activist, legal scholar, and author has made this book a must read for all of those interested in the development of the modern civil rights movement. One cannot truly understand and appreciate the intellectual and philosophical foundations of Black Power without reading this compelling book. It is a great and eloquent read that one cannot put down until completed. Professor Hamilton provides us with an honest and transparent look at the trials, travails, and triumphs of the talented Black men and women of his generation, which can serve as an example to all of us."
Dr. Robert T. Starks, Professor Emeritus of Political Science at Northeastern Illinois University's Carruthers Center for Inner City Studies and Founder of The Harold Washington Institute for Research and Policy Studies

Books Authored by Prof. Charles V. Hamilton

Black Power, The Politics of Liberation
(co-authored with Stokely Carmichael) (AKA Kwame Ture)
Random House, New York, 1967/1992

The Black Preacher in America
William Morrow Company, New York, 1972

The Bench and the Ballot, Southern Federal Judges and Black Voters
Oxford University Press, 1973

The Black Experience in American Politics
G.P. Putnam's Sons, New York, 1973

Adam Clayton Powell, Jr., The Political Biography of an American Dilemma
Macmillan Publishing Company, New York, 1991

The Dual Agenda
(co-authored with Dona C. Hamilton)
Columbia University Press, New York, 1997

"Professor Hamilton has demonstrated in this book a knack for using effective language and redemptive narrative to drive his point—the pursuit of social justice. Using the tool of professorship, Hamilton made his students appreciate the importance of being emancipation agents for advocates of civil rights and human dignity." You Can Use Yellow for Leaves is a must-read book.
Professor Levi Nwachuku, Lincoln University, Pennsylvania.

"You Can Use Yellow For Leaves, which refers to Hamilton's slightly older brother's counsel when he ran out of the green crayon (a Christmas gift from Santa Claus, [nee] his single mother), may be late in coming but is timely for having immeasurable value to all generations needing validation of the importance of sustaining the black struggle. In the early 70's, I worked with Professor Hamilton while a special projects consultant with the Columbia University Urban Center. The Center was engaged in bringing university departments into a closer collaboration with the nearby Harlem community residents and institutions. Professor Hamilton's memoir should be required reading for all who want to understand the making of a leading academic civil rights advocate and is a welcomed story about a hardy and heartfelt trek from a kitchenette on Southside Chicago to the highest realms of academia at prestigious Columbia University in New York City."
Everett Brandon, J.D., Commissioner Marin City, California

"Dr Charles V. Hamilton has given us a wonderful peek into his life and family. We get to experience the hopes and dreams of a young boy during the Depression nurtured by a mother who gave him a compass and a belief in the power of education and work. This is a story of a scholar, activist, husband and father whose journey takes him through the Black Power and Civil Rights movements in America, to the ending of the apartheid regime in South Africa, and more. Through these vignettes Dr. Hamilton reminds us of the importance of resilience at each step in life. We are privileged to see a life's work through the eyes of Dr. Hamilton."
Gerrard P. Bushell, CEO Dormitory Authority of the State of New York, PhD, Political Science, Columbia University